SPARKNOTES

Power Tactics

FOR THE NEW SAT

THE MATH SECTION
NUMBERS & OPERATIONS

D0104720

SPARK
NOTES

A DIVISION OF BARNES & NOBLE PUBLISHING

Spark Educational Publishing
A Division of Barnes & Noble Publishing
120 Fifth Avenue
New York, NY 10011

ISBN 1-4114-0276-6

Please submit changes or report errors to *www.sparknotes.com/errors*

Printed and bound in Canada.

SAT is a registered trademark of the College Entrance Examination Board, which was not involved in the production of, and does not endorse, this product.

Written by Jawad Ali

CONTENTS

INTRODUCTION

Truly effective SAT preparation doesn't need to be painful or time-consuming. SparkNotes' *Power Tactics for the New SAT* is proof that powerful test preparation can be streamlined so that you study only what you need. Instead of toiling away through a 700-page book or an expensive six-week course, you can choose the *Power Tactics* book that gets you where you want to be a lot sooner.

Perhaps you're Kid Math, the fastest number-slinger this side of the Mississippi, but a bit of a bumbler when it comes to words. Or maybe you've got the verbal parts down but can't seem to manage algebraic functions. *Power Tactics for the New SAT* provides an extremely focused review of every component on the new SAT, so you can design your own program of study.

If you're not exactly sure where you fall short, log on to **testprep.sparknotes.com/powertactics** and take our free diagnostic SAT test. This test will pinpoint your weaknesses and reveal exactly where to focus.

Since you're holding this book in your hands, it's pretty likely that SAT numbers & operations are what's giving you trouble. You've made the right decision, because in a few short hours, you will have mastered this part of the exam. No sweat, no major investment of time or money, no problem.

So, let's not waste any time: go forth and conquer SAT numbers & operations so you can get on with the *better parts* of your life!

ABOUT THE NEW SAT

THE OLD

The SAT, first administered in 1926, has undergone a thorough restructuring. For the last ten years, the SAT consisted of two sections: Verbal and Math. The Verbal section contained Analogies, Sentence Completions, and Critical Reading passages and questions. The Math section tested arithmetic, algebra, and geometry, as well as some probability, statistics, and data interpretation.

You received one point for each correct answer. For most questions, a quarter of a point was deducted for each incorrect answer. This was called the "wrong-answer penalty," which was designed to neutralize random guessing. If you simply filled in the bubble sheet at random, you'd likely get one-fifth of the items correct, given that each item has five answer choices (excluding student-produced–response items). You'd also get four-fifths of the items wrong, losing $4 \times {}^1/_4$, or 1 point for the four incorrectly answered items. Every time you determined an answer choice was wrong, you'd improve your odds by beating the wrong-answer penalty. The net number of points (less wrong-answer penalties) was called the "raw score."

Raw score = # of correct answers – $({}^1/_4 \times$ # of wrong answers)

That score was then converted to the familiar 200–800 "scaled score."

THE NEW

For 2005, the SAT added a Writing section and an essay, changed the name of *Verbal* to *Critical Reading*, and added algebra II content to the Math section. The following chart compares the old SAT with the new SAT:

Old SAT	New SAT
Verbal	**Critical Reading**
Analogies	*Eliminated*
Sentence Completions	Sentence Completions
Long Reading Passages	Long Reading Passages
Paired Reading Passages	Paired Reading Passages
	Short Reading Passages
Math—Question Types	
Multiple Choice	Multiple Choice
Quantitative Comparisons	*Eliminated*
Student-produced Responses	Student-produced Responses
Math—Content Areas	
Numbers & Operations	Numbers & Operations
Algebra I	Algebra I
	Algebra II
Geometry	Geometry
Data Analysis, Statistics & Probability	Data Analysis, Statistics & Probability
	Writing
	Identifying Sentence Errors
	Improving Sentences
	Improving Paragraphs
	Essay
Total Time: 3 hours	*Total Time*: 3 hours, 45 minutes
Maximum Scaled Score: 1600	*Maximum Scaled Score*: 2400 Separate Essay Score (2–12)

The scoring for the test is the same, except that the Writing section provides a third 200–800 scaled score, and there is now a separate essay score. The wrong-answer penalty is still in effect.

NEW PACKAGE, OLD PRODUCT

While the test has changed for test-*takers*, it has not changed all that much from the test-*maker*'s point of view. The Educational Testing Service (ETS) is a not-for-profit institute that creates the SAT for The College Board. Test creation is not as simple a task as you might think. Any standardized test question has to go through a rigorous series of editorial reviews and statistical studies before it can be released to the public. In fact, that's why the old SAT featured a seventh unscored, "experimental" section: new questions were introduced and tested out in these sections. ETS "feeds" potential questions to its test-takers to measure the level of difficulty. Given the complex and lengthy process of developing new questions, it would be impossible for ETS to introduce *totally* new question types or make major changes to the existing question types.

Now that you know these facts, the "new" SAT will start to make more sense. The changes were neither random nor unexpected. Actually, the only truly *new* question type on the SAT is the short reading passage followed by a couple of questions. However, the skills tested and strategies required are virtually identical to the tried-and-true long reading-passage question type. All other additions to the test consist of new *content*, rather than new *question types*. Both multiple-choice and student-produced–response math questions ("grid-ins") will now feature algebra II concepts. Same question type, new content. Critical Reading features one fiction passage per test, as well as questions on genre, rhetorical devices, and cause and effect. Same question type, different content.

Even the much-feared new Writing section is in a sense old news. The PSAT and the SAT II Writing tests have featured exactly the same multiple-choice question types for years. The essay format and scoring rubric are virtually identical to those of the SAT II Writing test. The College Board had no other choice, given how long the test-development process is.

The other major changes are omissions, not additions: Quantitative Comparisons and Analogies have been dumped from the test.

So, in a nutshell, ETS has simply attached an SAT II Writing test to the old SAT, dropped Analogies and Quantitative Comparisons, added some Algebra II content and short reading passages, and ensured that some fiction and fiction-related questions are included. That's it.

A USER'S GUIDE

Reading this book will maximize your score on SAT numbers & operations questions. We've divided up your study into two sections: **Power Tactics** and **Practice Sets**. The Power Tactics will provide you with important concepts and the strategies you'll need to tackle numbers & operations on the SAT. The Practice Sets will give you an opportunity to apply what you learn to SAT questions. To achieve your target score, you'll learn:

- The two question types you'll encounter: multiple-choice and student-produced response, as well as the subtypes: **Math Head**, **Supermath Head**, **Numbers Game**, and **The Real World**.
- What the test-makers are actually trying to test with each numbers & operations question type
- Essential concepts and powerful step methods to maximize your score
- Test-taking strategies that allow you to approach each section with the best possible mindset
- The 8 most common mistakes and how to avoid them

In order to get the most out of this book:

- Make sure to read each section thoroughly and carefully.
- Don't skip the Guided Practice questions.
- Read all explanations to all questions.
- Go to **testprep.sparknotes.com/powertactics** for a free full-length diagnostic **pretest**. This test will help you determine your strengths and weaknesses for numbers & operations and for the entire SAT.
- Go back to our website after you complete this book to take a **posttest**. This test will tell you how well you've mastered SAT numbers & operations and what topics you still need to review.

THE POWER
TACTICS

ANATOMY OF SAT NUMBERS & OPERATIONS

Even without reading this book or preparing for the SAT in any way, you'd still get some numbers & operations problems right. However, there's a big difference between:

1. Sweating out a problem, breathing a sigh of relief when you finish it, and timidly moving on.
2. Answering a problem, seeing that the next problem contains a bunch of pushover terms, such as **sets** and **ratios**, and licking your chops in expectation of an easy mark.

Moving from scenario 1 to scenario 2 is not as tough as you might imagine. It just takes a little bit of work. The mistake many students make is taking the SAT cold. That's right—no preparation. Not so much as a flip through the information booklet.

By familiarizing yourself with every type of numbers & operations question you can encounter on the SAT, you can approach each question coolly and calmly, knowing in advance what needs to be done to answer it correctly. It's about switching from survival mode to attack mode. It's attack mode that will help you score high.

In this section we provide you with an X-ray of SAT numbers & operations. Later on, we'll review the subtypes of questions and specific strategies for approaching each one. By looking at these questions inside and out, you'll know more about how The College Board tests your skills and how to approach each and every question you'll encounter on the test.

There are two types of math questions on the SAT: multiple-choice and student-produced response.

MULTIPLE CHOICE

Here is a typical multiple-choice question and the terms we'll use to refer to its various parts:

Find a solution: $\dfrac{(14-2) \times 3}{2} + 7 - (3-1)^2 =$

(A) -2
(B) -3
(C) 6
(D) -6
(E) 8

The sentence containing the question is the **stem**. The lettered options below the stem are the **answer choices**. Numerical answer choices are always listed in order from smallest to largest or largest to smallest. Only one of these answer choices is correct; the other four answers are called **distractors**, because that's exactly what they're designed to do: *distract* attention from the correct answer. The stem and the answer choices grouped together are called an **item**. An entire multiple-choice section, comprised of several items, is called a **set**.

STUDENT-PRODUCED RESPONSE

Student-produced response is The College Board's way of saying, "Do it yourself, Bub." Simply put, you, the student, must supply the correct answer without choosing from a group of answer choices. Answering student-produced responses requires filling in a grid like the one shown below. Therefore, we refer to these questions as **grid-ins**:

Directions for Student-Produced Response Questions

Each of the remaining 15 questions requires you to solve the problem and enter your answer by marking the ovals in the special grid, as shown in the examples below.

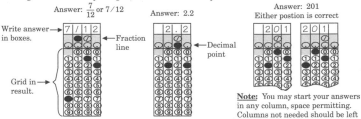

Answer: $\frac{7}{12}$ or $7/12$

Answer: 2.2

Answer: 201
Either postion is correct

Write answer in boxes.

←Fraction line

←Decimal point

Grid in result.

Note: You may start your answers in any column, space permitting. Columns not needed should be left blank.

• Mark no more than one oval in any column.

• Because the answer sheet will be machine-scored, **you will receive credit only if the ovals are filled in completely.**

• Although not required, it is suggested that you write your answer in the boxes at the top of the columns to help you fill in the ovals accurately.

• Some problems may have more than one correct answer. In such cases, grid only one answer

• No question has a negative answer.

• **Mixed numbers** such as $2\frac{1}{2}$ must be gridded as 2.5 or 5/2 If [2 1 / 2] is gridded, it will be interpreted as $\frac{21}{2}$, not $2\frac{1}{2}$.)

• <u>**Decimal Accuracy:**</u> If you obtain a decimal answer, **enter the most accurate value the grid will accommodate.** For example, if you obtain an answer such as 0.6666 . . . , you should record the result as .666 or .667. **Less accurate values such as .66 or .67 are not acceptable.** Acceptable ways to grid $\frac{2}{3} = .666 \ldots$

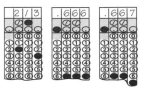

An example of a grid-in might be:

9. If $a^4 > a^5$, what is one possible value of a?

The grid is fairly self-explanatory. If you work out an item and the answer is 2, you write 2 in the space, then fill in the "2" oval underneath. There are also decimal points and fraction bars in case your answer is not a whole number. We refer to an individual grid-in as an **item**. A complete grid-in section, comprised of items, is called a **set**.

There are three peculiar things about grid-ins:

1. **There may be more than one correct answer to each item.** You're probably stuck in the "only one correct choice" mindset brought on by excessive multiple-choice preparation. But don't let this paralyze you: if you get more than one correct answer, pick one, grid it in, and move on to the next item.

2. **Answers can never be negative numbers.** Although there is more than one possible answer, there is actually a limit to what you can grid in.

There is no way to denote negative numbers on a grid-in. Why? Who knows, and who cares for that matter? The fact is that all grid-ins must be positive (or zero, which is neither negative nor positive). So if you come up with more than one correct answer, be sure to choose one that is a positive number. If all your answers are negative, you have made a mistake in working out the item.

3. **Improper fractions must be simplified or converted to a decimal answer.** Let's say you come up with $1\frac{1}{2}$ as the answer to an item. If you grid the answer in as $1\frac{1}{2}$, the computer that scans your answer sheet will read your answer as $\frac{11}{2}$. To avoid getting this item wrong, convert the improper fraction into the plain old fraction $\frac{3}{2}$ or the decimal 1.5.

KEY FORMULAS

Math sets on the SAT provide you with key geometric formulas in a reference area that looks like this:

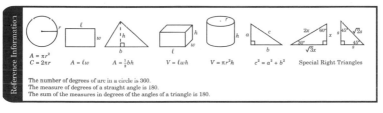

The reference area always appears at the beginning of the set, below the instructions.

WHAT THE SAT COVERS

Numbers & operations items on the new SAT Math section test the following broad concepts:

- Number terms
- Order of operations
- Odd and even numbers
- Positive and negative numbers
- Divisibility and remainders
- Factors
- Multiples
- Fractions

- Decimals
- Percents
- Ratios
- Exponents
- Roots and radicals
- Sequences
- Sets

Some of these concepts might not be familiar to you. Don't sweat it: that's why you're reading this book!

ORDER OF DIFFICULTY

The number of the item clues you in to whether it's an easy (low number) or hard (high number) item. Sample items in this section have numbers between 1 and 20 that approximate where the item would appear on a real SAT Math section. Make sure to note the number of the item before tackling it. We cover order of difficulty in more detail in the Test-Taking Strategies section.

ESSENTIAL
CONCEPTS

If SAT numbers & operations were a radio station, then this section would be the top-forty countdown. It's not going to include every fact, just the ones that get the most airplay on the new SAT. When we describe a concept, we cover only the numbers & operations you need to solve SAT items.

You want to have this knowledge down cold. The better you know it, the easier your life will be.

NUMBER TERMS

To answer the items correctly, you need to be familiar with the terminology of numbers. These terms appear in a majority of all SAT Math items, not just the ones dealing with numbers & operations.

Number Terms and Definitions

Term	Definition	Examples
Whole numbers	The set of numbers we use to count objects.	0, 1, 2, 3
Natural numbers	The set of all whole numbers, excluding zero.	1, 2, 3, 4, 5, 6
Integers	The set of all positive and negative whole numbers, including zero. No fractions.	−2, −1, 0, 1, 2, 3

Term	Definition	Examples
Rational Numbers	The set of numbers that can be expressed as integers in fractions, in the form m/n, where m and n are integers.	$\frac{3}{4}, \frac{1}{2}, \frac{5}{6}$
Irrational numbers	The set of all numbers that cannot be expressed as integers in a fraction.	$\sqrt{2}$, 0.33333333, π
Real numbers	Every number on the number line. The set of real numbers includes all rational and irrational numbers.	Anything!

ORDER OF OPERATIONS

Math is all about rules. You can't go around saying $2 + 3 = 87$. You have to follow rules when adding, subtracting, multiplying, dividing, or squaring. The order of mathematical operations is commonly known as **PEMDAS**. This nifty acronym shows the order in which mathematical operations should be performed as you work through an expression or equation.

- **P**arentheses
- **E**xponents
- **M**ultiplication
- **D**ivision
- **A**ddition
- **S**ubtraction

There is a small catch to the last two steps of PEMDAS. Once you're left with addition and subtraction, you move *from left to right* in the equation.

Let's take old PEMDAS out for a spin.

$$\frac{5(5-2)^2}{5} - 3 + 2(3-1) =$$

First, work out the stuff in the parentheses:

$$\frac{5(3)^2}{5} - 3 + 2(2) =$$

Then do the exponents:

$$\frac{5 \times 9}{5} - 3 + 2(2) =$$

Now multiply like wild dogs are chasing you:

$$\frac{45}{5} - 3 + 4 =$$

Next, calmly divide anything that needs dividing:

$$9 - 3 + 4 =$$

Then do the addition and subtraction, moving from left to right:

10

ODD AND EVEN NUMBERS

Even numbers are numbers that divide by 2 without leaving a remainder. **Odd numbers** are the numbers that, when divided by 2, leave a remainder of 1. The only number that might cause you to scratch your head is zero. It turns out that zero is, in fact, even.

So zero is the only number that has a strange property in terms of odd and even. How often do you think zero *just happens* to appear on the SAT?

Operations and Odd and Even Numbers

Now that you've been introduced to odd and even numbers, it's time to get down to business. You have to know how to add, subtract, multiply, and divide odd and even numbers:

Addition	Subtraction	Multiplication
even + even = even	even − even = even	even × even = even
odd + odd = even	odd − odd = even	odd × odd = odd
even + odd = odd	even − odd = odd	even × odd = even
odd + even = odd	odd − even = oddd	odd × even = even

Knowing these general rules makes it easier for you to eliminate answer choices on multiple-choice items. If you know your answer needs to be an odd number, for instance, you should be able to eliminate all the even-numbered answer choices.

POSITIVE/NEGATIVE/UNDECIDED

Here's an example of a number line:

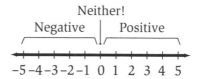

Negative numbers can mess with your head. Looking at the number line, you can see that –2 is greater than –5, but your mind doesn't like this because it's used to positive numbers, and 5 is greater than 2. The SAT loves to set traps like this using negative numbers. Be vigilant.

You also need to know how multiplying and dividing negative numbers affect an equation. Study this chart and memorize the eight possible combinations:

Multiplication	Division
positive × positive = positive	positive ÷ positive = positive
negative × negative = positive	negative ÷ negative = positive
positive × negative = negative	positive ÷ negative = negative
negative × positive = negative	negative ÷ positive = negative

Negative Numbers

An item that includes negative numbers and parentheses can be tricky:

1. $4 + 2 - (2 - 6) =$

When you see a negative sign before parentheses, you need to *distribute* the negative across the parentheses. So $-(2 - 6)$ becomes $-2 + 6$:

$$4 + 2 - (2 - 6) =$$

$$4 + 2 - 2 + 6 = 10$$

Absolute Value

The cure to negative numbers is **absolute value**. The absolute value of a number is the distance between any given number on the number line and zero. This distance is never negative. If you're traveling from 3, the distance from 3 to zero is three spaces. If you're traveling from –3 to zero, the distance is also 3 spaces, so the absolute value of –3 is 3. So for positive numbers, the absolute value is the same as the number itself. For negative numbers, the absolute value is the positive version of that number.

Absolute value is written using two thin bars: $|{-3}| = 3$

In an equation, absolute value brackets work like positive parentheses. You have to work whatever's inside the absolute value brackets first, but if you get a negative number, you have to convert it to a positive number when taking it out of the absolute value brackets.

$$-2 \times |5 - 6| + 7 =$$
$$-2 \times |{-1}| + 7 =$$
$$-2 \times 1 + 7 =$$
$$-2 + 7 = 5$$

DIVISIBILITY AND REMAINDERS

This is division, old-school style. Actually, division, grade-school style is probably more accurate. There are a bunch of **divisibility** rules that you learned in grade school, then quickly forgot. The SAT dusts them off and showcases them in an item or two, so here's a trip down memory lane:

1. All whole numbers are divisible by 1.
2. A number that ends in an even digit is divisible by 2.
3. A number is divisible by 3 if its digits add up to a number divisible by 3. For example, 384 is divisible by 3 because $3 + 8 + 4 = 15$, and 15 is divisible by 3.
4. A number is divisible by 4 if its last two digits are divisible by 4. The number 5,764 is divisible by 4 because 64 is divisible by 4.
5. A number is divisible by 5 if it ends in 0 or 5.
6. A number is divisible by 6 if it is even and divisible by 3. This rule is a combo of rules 2 and 3.
7. Sadly, there is no rule for 7.
8. A number is divisible by 8 if its last three digits are divisible by 8. For example, 1,249,216 is divisible by 8 because 216 is divisible by 8.

9. A number is divisible by 9 if its digits add up to a number divisible by 9. The number 2,952 is divisible by 9 because 2 + 9 + 5 + 2 = 18.

10. A number is divisible by 10 if it ends in 0.

Remainders

When all of us have calculators embedded in our forearms, **remainders** will finally become extinct. Until then, remainders will continue their marginalized existence. A remainder is the integer left over after one number has been divided into another. In the following example, the remainder is 3, and the dividend is 4:

$$
7 \overline{)\begin{array}{r} 4\,r3 \\ 31 \\ -28 \\ \hline 3 \end{array}}
$$

Because you get to use a calculator on the exam and because remainders show up as fractions or decimals on calculators, the SAT includes one or two remainder items to trick you up.

FEARLESS FACTORS

An integer is called a **factor** if it divides another integer evenly. For example, 3 is one of the factors of 6, because $6 \div 3 = 2$.

There's no magic formula to determine the factors of any given number, although the divisibility rule on the previous page can help. For example, for the number 576, you know that the following numbers are factors:

- 2 is a factor because 6 is even.
- 3 is a factor because 5 + 7 + 6 = 18, which is divisible by 3.
- 6 is a factor because 2 and 3 are factors.

All even numbers have 2 as a factor. Lucky them. All **prime numbers** have two and only two factors: 1 and the number itself. Think of prime numbers as loners of sorts. The number 2 is the only even prime number. All other prime numbers are odd.

Prime Factorization

As its name suggests, prime factorization involves using **prime factors**. Prime factorization is like taking apart a bicycle until you have every individual piece as small as it can get: the chain, the seat, the handlebars, and so forth. To find the prime factorization of a number, you divide it and all its factors until every remaining integer is a prime number. The easiest way to solve for prime factorization is to make a pretty little tree:

4.   What is the prime factorization of 72?

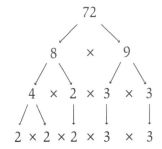

Throw some tinsel on that tree, and you've got yourself a Christmas party.

MULTIPLES, MULTIPLES, MULTIPLES

Keep in mind that mathematicians are a literal bunch. So if you come across a concept called **multiples**, you can guess that multiplication is going to play a big part in it.

The multiples of an integer are the product of that integer and another integer. Consider the number 7. Some multiples of 7 are:

$$7 \times 2 = 14$$

$$7 \times 5 = 35$$

$$7 \times 8 = 56$$

$$7 \times 100 = 700$$

$$7 \times 247 = 1729$$

If you have two different numbers, you may be asked to find the **least common multiple** (LCM) the two numbers share. The LCM of two numbers is defined as the smallest integer that is a multiple of both numbers. Sometimes the LCM is simply the two numbers multiplied together. The LCM of 7 and 5 is 35, for instance. This is because 7 and 5 are both prime numbers. However, the LCM of 12 and 10 is not 120. To find the LCM of these two numbers, we have to run some numbers through the factor machine:

Multiples of 10	Multiples of 12
10	12
20	24
30	36
40	48
50	60
60	72
70	84
80	96
90	108
100	120
110	
120	

Can you see a number less than 120 that both numbers have in common? If you don't, you must have some vision problem that makes the number 60 invisible to you. 60 is the LCM of 10 and 12.

There's a complicated mathematical method to determine LCM, and there's the way shown above. On the SAT, take the easy route.

FRACTIONS

Fractions are *ubiquitous* on the SAT Math section (*there's* an SAT word for you to chew on). A fraction shows the relationship between a part of something and the whole of something. Here's what a fraction looks like: $\frac{2}{3}$.

A fraction is composed of two numbers, a numerator, and a denominator. The **numerator** (the *part*) is above the fraction bar, and the **denominator** (the *whole*) is below it. So in our example, 2 is the numerator, and 3 is the denominator.

What if we multiply both the numerator and the denominator of $\frac{2}{3}$ by 4? We would end up with:

$$\frac{2}{3} \times \frac{4}{4} = \frac{8}{12}$$

Because we multiplied both parts by the same numbers, the two fractions ($\frac{2}{3}$ and $\frac{8}{12}$) have the same part-to-whole relationship. These fractions are **equivalent fractions**, which means they equal each other.

Suppose we decide that $\frac{8}{12}$ is too bulky. We know that 8 and 12 have an LCM of 4—remember that term?—so we can whittle that $\frac{8}{12}$ down to a slimmer fraction:

$$\frac{8}{12} = \frac{8 \div 4}{12 \div 4} = \frac{2}{3}$$

Taking a fat fraction and dividing out similar terms from both the numerator and denominator is called **reducing** a fraction.

Reducing fractions and making equivalent fractions are necessary skills, because you often have to perform these tasks before adding, subtracting, multiplying, or dividing fractions. Don't simply take our word for it. Review the following sections.

Adding and Subtracting Fractions

We'll start simple. Fractions with the same denominators are the easiest. You need only add or subtract the numerators:

$$\frac{2}{5} + \frac{3}{5} = \frac{5}{5} = 1$$
$$\frac{2}{5} - \frac{3}{5} = -\frac{1}{5}$$

No rocket science there. Fractions with different denominators are one degree trickier. Before adding or subtracting them, you first need to make sure that the denominators are the same.

For instance, if you need to perform the operation $\frac{2}{3} - \frac{4}{15}$, first you have to equalize the denominators of these two fractions. You do this by finding the lowest common multiple of denominators 3 and 15. This number is the **lowest common denominator**, or LCD.

$$15 = 3 \times 5$$
$$3 = 3 \times 1$$

Because 15 is a multiple of 3, the LCD is 15. So all you need to do is multiply 3 and 5 to get 15. However, if you increase the denominator by 5, you need to increase the numerator by 5 too. Remember: all fractions are the parts of a whole:

$$\frac{2}{3} \times \frac{5}{5} = \frac{2 \times 5}{3 \times 5} = \frac{10}{15}$$

Now you can get your subtraction on:

$$\frac{10}{15} - \frac{4}{15} = \frac{6}{15}$$

Suppose the LCD is difficult to find, such as when you have 12 and 18 in the denominator. You could simply multiply 12 and 18 and use the product as a common denominator. This gives you some big fractions that you have to reduce. Working with big numbers increases the possibility of errors, so it's best to find the LCD before proceeding.

Multiplying and Dividing Fractions

Compared to adding and subtracting with different denominators, multiplying fractions is easy. You just find the product of the fractions' denominators and numerators:

$$\frac{2}{3} \times \frac{4}{5} = \frac{2 \times 4}{3 \times 5} = \frac{8}{15}$$

Sometimes you can **cross-cancel** numbers and make multiplying even simpler. In the example below, the 5 in the numerator takes out the 5 in the denominator.

$$\frac{5}{7} \times \frac{4}{5} = \frac{\cancel{5}}{7} \times \frac{4}{\cancel{5}} = \frac{4}{7}$$

Division of fractions is just like multiplication of fractions with a little twist. When dividing, you flip the second fraction, then multiply:

$$\frac{2}{3} \div \frac{5}{6} = \frac{2}{3} \times \frac{6}{5} = \frac{12}{15} = \frac{4}{5}$$

One key concept to remember is: when you multiply a fraction by itself, the resulting fraction is less than the original fraction. For example:

$$\frac{1}{2} \times \frac{1}{2} = \frac{1}{4}$$

The fraction $\frac{1}{4}$ is smaller than $\frac{1}{2}$.

Weird-Looking Fractions

Not every fraction on the SAT is in the button-down conservative style. Many items are designed to freak you out. To do this, the SAT uses **mixed numbers** and **complex fractions**. We'll cover complex fractions first.

For complex fractions, you have to calculate a fraction of a fraction:

$$\frac{\frac{2 \times 4}{3}}{\frac{1}{2}}$$

See that bar between the 3 and the 1? It's a fraction bar, but you can also think of it as a division sign. That bar holds the key to solving complex fractions. Take the fraction above the bar and divide it by the fraction below the bar. You just learned how to divide fractions, so this shouldn't be tough:

$$\frac{\frac{2 \times 4}{3}}{\frac{1}{2}} = \frac{2 \times 4}{3} \div \frac{1}{2} = \frac{2 \times 4}{3} \times \frac{2}{1} = \frac{8}{3} \times \frac{2}{1} = \frac{16}{3}$$

Simple enough. On to mixed numbers.

A mixed number, or **improper fraction**, includes both an integer and a fraction. For example, $2\frac{1}{2}$ is a mixed number. Mixed numbers are impenetrable to simple addition and subtraction, so you need to do one of two things before you work with them:

1. Convert them into proper fractions.
2. Use your calculator and change them to decimals.

Converting improper fractions is pretty simple. Start with a mixed number, such as $4\frac{2}{7}$. Multiply the integer 4 by the denominator 7, then add that product to the numerator 2 and place the new number over the old denominator:

$$4\frac{2}{7} = \frac{4 \times 7 + 2}{7} = \frac{28 + 2}{7} = \frac{30}{7}$$

Remember that on the grid-in section, you cannot write a mixed number as your answer because the computer reads $4\frac{2}{7}$ as $\frac{42}{7}$. That's why converting mixed numbers becomes so important. Of course, you can also just convert the whole mess into a decimal.

DECIMALS

A **decimal** is a fraction that's been churned through your calculator. If you take any fraction and divide the numerator by the denominator, what comes out is a decimal equivalent to the starting fraction:

$$\frac{5}{8} = 5 \div 8 = 0.625$$

The decimal value 0.625 is the same as $\frac{5}{8}$. It's another way of writing a part to a whole. On the SAT, flipping between fractions and decimals is a handy skill. You've seen how to change a fraction to a decimal. To change a decimal to a fraction, follow the three steps below.

1. Remove the decimal point and make the decimal number the numerator.

If we start with 0.862, we place the 862 in the numerator:

$$\frac{862}{?}$$

2. Let the denominator be the number 1, followed by as many zeroes as there are decimal places after the decimal point.

There are three decimal places after the zero in 0.862, so we'll want to put three zeroes after the 1:

$$\frac{862}{?} = \frac{862}{1000}$$

3. Reduce the fraction.

Find a common factor and reduce the number:

$$\frac{862}{1000} = \frac{862 \div 2}{1000 \div 2} = \frac{431}{500}$$

PERCENTS

If math terms formed cliques, then percents, decimals, and fractions would all hang out together. **Percent** is one more way to represent a part of a whole. The word itself means "of 100" in Latin, so a percent represents some part of the number 100, which is the whole.

Converting a decimal to a percent is simple: take the decimal and move the decimal point two spaces to the right. Then add the lovely % symbol. The number is now a percentage. For example, the decimal 0.62 becomes 62%, and the decimal 0.087 becomes 8.7%. If you have to convert a percent into a decimal, just go the other way and move the decimal point two spaces to the left. So 78% becomes 0.78. How easy is that?

Flipping between percents and fractions is all about using 100 as the denominator. Recall that *percent* means "of 100," so 65% means 65 of 100, or $\frac{65}{100}$. Taking a percent and placing it over 100 does the trick of converting it into a fraction, although often you still have to reduce:

$$\frac{65}{100} = \frac{65 \div 5}{100 \div 5} = \frac{13}{20}$$

To change a fraction into a percent, you have to turn the denominator to 100. The numerator then becomes the percent. Let's use $\frac{3}{4}$ as an example. To get the denominator equal to 100, we have to multiply by 25:

$$\frac{3}{4} \times \frac{25}{25} = \frac{75}{100} = 75\%$$

That covers all the different ways to switch between fractions, percents, and decimals. It's good stuff to know, because many SAT items like to test this conversion process in one way or another.

Percents in Word Problems

SAT word problems often use convoluted wording to ask for percents. Let's inoculate ourselves against these wicked temptations. The typical percent word problem will say something like:

11. 4 is what percent of 10?

Here's what each term means in Mathspeak:

Term	Mathspeak
is	=
what	insert a variable
percent	divide by 100
of	multiply

Using this chart, "4 is what percent of 10?" transforms to:

$$4 = \frac{w}{100}(10)$$
$$4 = \frac{10w}{100}$$
$$4 = \frac{w}{10}$$
$$40 = w$$

4 is 40% of 10.

Percents Up and Down

Percents can be tricky. Consider this situation. There's one person in the room. Another walks in. The percentage increase is 100%, because there are now 100% more people in the room. You can use the following formula to calculate percent change:

$$\text{Percent change} = \frac{\text{difference}}{\text{original number}} \times 100$$

Now suppose a person leaves. What's the percentage decrease? Many people jump and say 100%, but percents don't work that way. The actual percentage decrease is 50%, because exactly half (one out of two) of the people who were in the room left. The number of people who left the room is the same as the number of people who entered, but the percent change is different because the original amounts are different. Using our formula:

$$\text{Percent change} = \frac{1}{2} \times 100 = 50\%$$

If this were an SAT item, you can bet that 100% would have been a distractor.

Consider the following item:

8. The original factory price of a pencil is $5. The Tall Mouse art store buys the pencil at the original price, then sells it at a profit of 10%. A starving artist in Santa Monica buys the pencil at the art store, then decides to reduce the price at which he bought the pencil by 25% and sell it to his even more starving student. In dollars, approximately how much does the student pay for the pencil?

(A) $4.13
(B) $4.40
(C) $4.50
(D) $5.50
(E) $6.75

For an item like this, you have to calculate the result of two successive price changes. To do this, you need to remember that the final price depends on the previous price change.

So let's calculate the first price increase. To do this, find 10% of $5:

$$\frac{10}{100} \times 5 = \$0.50$$

Now add $0.50 to the original price of the pencil:

$$\$5 + \$0.50 = \$5.50$$

Now find 25% of 5.50.

$$\frac{25}{100} \times 5.5 = \$1.375$$

This is the amount the art teacher reduced the pencil's price. When we subtract 1.375 from 5.5, we should have the final price:

$$\$5.50 - \$1.375 = \$4.125 \approx \$4.13$$

That's answer **A**.

Be careful while solving double percent items, because the SAT writers love to set traps. For instance, if you reason that because the first price increase is 10% and the second price decrease is 25%, the net decrease is 15%, you are falling into a classic SAT trap.

RATIOS

Math teachers love to use pizza slices to teach fractions and ratios. Who are we to argue with tradition? Consider a humble eight-slice pizza. You eat three pieces, and your imaginary buddy, Kronhorst, eats the other five. (Imaginary friends don't have to worry about gaining weight.) The fraction of the pizza you ate can be determined by the *part* you ate over the *whole* number of slices. That's what fractions are, a part to a whole.

Ratios compare parts to parts. The ratio of pieces you ate to the pieces Kronhorst ate is 3:5, because it compares the part you ate to the part Kronhorst ate. The ratio can be written as 3:5 or $\frac{3}{5}$ or *ratio of 3 to 5*. Even though $\frac{3}{5}$ looks like a fraction, it's not. The bottom number is *not* a denominator.

If the ratio of A to B is 3:4, this does not necessarily mean that there are 3 pieces of A and 4 pieces of B. There could be 6 pieces of A and 8 pieces of B for a ratio of 6:8, which then reduces down to 3:4. Ratios don't always tell you the actual amount, but they do allow you to compare one object to another:

2. For every 50 Americans who buy books online, 10 buy books at bookstores. What's the ratio of those who buy books online to those who buy books at bookstores?

(A) 1:2
(B) 50:25
(C) 4:1
(D) 5:1
(E) 5:6

First find the ratio of those who buy books online to those who buy books at bookstores. This ratio can be written as 50:10.

You can simplify ratios the same way fractions are simplified:

$50:10 = 5:1$, choice **D**.

For every 5 people who buy books online, 1 person actually goes to the bookstore and buys a book. Whether that person actually reads it is another issue.

Proportions

Some items not only require knowledge of ratios but also test your ability to figure out the actual values from the ratios.

For instance, look at this item:

4. At a computer company in Brooklyn, the ratio of people who wear black, gray, and brown ties is 7:5:3. If the total number of workers is 45, how many workers wear gray ties?

(A) 3
(B) 5
(C) 9
(D) 15
(E) 21

You immediately know that for every 5 gray ties there are 7 black ones and 3 brown ones. You also know that for every 15 ties $(7 + 5 + 3)$, 5 ties are gray and that the total number of ties is 45. Keep in mind that the ratios do not change, no matter the total number of objects. This helps you set up a **proportion**—an equation based on the notion that two ratios are equal.

$5:15$ is the same as $x:45$. To solve for x:

$$\frac{5}{15} = \frac{x}{45}$$

Now cross multiply to get:

$$45 \times 5 = 15 \times x$$

$$225 = 15x$$

$$x = 15$$

The total number of gray ties is 15, choice **D**.

EXPONENTS, OR THE POWERS THAT BE

The word *exponent* means "tiny raised number." That's not 100% mathematically accurate, but it's true from a totally visual standpoint.

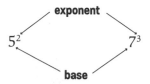

An **exponent** above a number tells you how many times that number has to be multiplied by itself. For the number on the left above, the **base** is 5 and the exponent is 2. This means we must multiply the base of 5 by itself twice:

$$5^2 = (5)(5) = 25$$

When the exponent is 2, you can also use the term **squared** to describe the expression. In the above example, 5 squared is 25. The number 25 is a **perfect square** because it is the product of an integer squared. The first ten perfect squares are:

$$1^2 = 1$$
$$2^2 = 4$$
$$3^2 = 9$$
$$4^2 = 16$$
$$5^2 = 25$$
$$6^2 = 36$$
$$7^2 = 49$$
$$8^2 = 64$$
$$9^2 = 81$$
$$10^2 = 100$$

When the exponent is 3, you can say the base is being **cubed**:

$$7^3 = (7)(7)(7) = 343$$

So 7 cubed is 343. One other way to talk about exponents is to use the term **power** when describing the exponent. Five squared can also be called "five to the second power" or "five to the power of two," and 7 cubed can be called "seven to the third power" or "seven to the power of three."

Now that you understand the basic terms, let's start messing with exponents.

Adding and Subtracting Powers: A Big No-No

Numbers with exponents cannot be simply added or subtracted. If you see $7^2 + 3^2$, it would be easy to say the answer is 10^2. It would also be quite wrong:

$$7^2 + 3^2 = (7)(7) + (3)(3) = 49 + 9 = 58$$

whereas

$$10^2 = (10)(10) = 100$$

To add or subtract numbers with exponents, compute the values of the numbers first, then add:

$$3^2 + 2^2 + 8^2 = (3)(3) + (2)(2) + (8)(8) = 9 + 4 + 64 = 77$$

If the base *and* the exponent are the same, you can add or subtract expressions. For instance, in the expression $3y^4 + 8y^4$, both terms have the same base (the variable y) and the same exponent (4). Therefore, you can express it as: $3y^4 + 8y^4 = 11y^4$

When algebraic expressions have different bases or different exponents, you cannot add or subtract.

Multiplying and Dividing Powers: Yeah, That's Allowed

Think about how the term s^3 is just shorthand for $(s)(s)(s)$. The term s^4 is shorthand for $(s)(s)(s)(s)$. If you multiply these two terms together, you're really just adding the exponents together:

$$s^3 \times s^4 = (s)(s)(s) \times (s)(s)(s)(s) = s^7 = s^{3+4}$$

If you have the same base, you can add exponents together when multiplying. When dividing, you can subtract them, but again, the bases have to be exactly the same:

$$\frac{r^{11}}{r^7} = r^{(11-7)} = r^4$$

$$x^7 \div x^3 = x^{(7-3)} = x^4$$

The Freaky Exponent Stuff

Because the new SAT wants to emphasize some of the more obscure corners of the math world, you can expect the test to set some traps using unusual exponents.

One of these traps comes in the form of raising a power to a power, $(3^2)^3$. This is "three squared then cubed," for those who like the lingo. To simplify it, all you have to do is multiply the exponents:

$$(3^2)^3 = 3^{(2 \times 3)} = 3^6$$

If you want to understand why this works, write out all the 3s involved, and you'll come up with the same answer.

Negative numbers, in both the base and exponents, are another way the SAT tries to trap you. When you raise a negative base number to a power (or multiply it by itself), you may have to change the sign of the number:

$$(-3)^2 = 9, \text{ because } (-3)(-3) = 9$$

A negative number remains negative when raised to an odd exponent:

$$(-3)^3 = -(27, \text{ because } (-3)(-3)(-3)) = -27$$

If you have a negative exponent, first make it positive, then make that new number the denominator of a fraction with 1 as the numerator.

$$5^{-4} = \frac{1}{5^4}$$

What if the exponent is a fraction? (We told you the test is filled with fractions.) If that's the case, the numerator becomes the power to which the number is raised, and the denominator is the **root** of the number.

$$x^{\frac{a}{b}} = (\sqrt[b]{x})^a$$

The symbol $\sqrt{}$ is called a **radical**, and anything under the radical is called a **radicand**. Here's an example of a fractional exponent:

$$16^{\frac{3}{4}} = (\sqrt[4]{16})^3 = 8$$

Want to know more about roots and radicals? Well, we won't keep you waiting.

ROOTS AND RADICALS

Roots are the flip side of exponents, just as division is the flip side of multiplication. When you square a number, you multiply it by itself. So 5 squared is $(5)(5) = 25$. Square roots go in the opposite direction. To get the square root of 25, you need to find the number that when multiplied by itself equals 25. The answer is 5.

$$5 \times 5 = 25, \text{ therefore } \sqrt{25} = 5$$

The SAT is very fond of square roots, but you should know how to work with other roots as well. The basic concept is this:

To calculate the value of $\sqrt[b]{a}$, you have to find a number that, when multiplied by itself b times, gives a:

$$\sqrt[4]{81} = 3, \text{ because } 3^4 = 81$$

Roots are similar to exponents in two other ways:

1. **Addition/Subtraction.** Can you add or subtract exponents? Nope. The same is true for roots. You cannot just add or subtract them. You have to work out each root separately. Only then can you add or subtract:

$$\sqrt{9} - \sqrt{4} = 3 - 2 = 1$$

2. **Multiplication/Division.** As with exponents, this is allowed. If the roots are of the same degree, you can multiply and divide two roots by simply multiplying or dividing the numbers under the radical sign:

$$\sqrt{a} \times \sqrt{b} = \sqrt{ab}$$

$$\sqrt{a} \div \sqrt{b} = \sqrt{\frac{a}{b}}$$

$$\sqrt{6} \div \sqrt{2} = \sqrt{\frac{6}{2}} = \sqrt{3}$$

SEQUENCES

A **sequence** can be described as a series of numbers that proceed one after another in a certain pattern. Think of that cheerleader chant that starts with "2, 4, 6, 8!" Before you ask who we appreciate, realize that those four numbers form a sequence wherein the next term is two more than the previous term.

Fortunately, you don't need an intimate knowledge of pom-pom maintenance and usage to understand sequences.

Arithmetic Sequence

In an **arithmetic sequence**, each term is greater than the previous term by some fixed constant. In our cheerleader cheer, the first term equals 2, and the interval is 2:

$$2, 4, 6, 8, \ldots$$

The value by which the sequence increases remains the same. This term is called the **constant**. In this case, the constant—often called k—equals 2.

There are many different formulas regarding sequences, but you're usually better off just using your pencil and calculator to solve most SAT sequence items. Write out the sequence until you find what you need. It may seem low-tech, but it brings results, and that's all that really counts.

Geometric Sequence and Exponential Growth

Arithmetic sequences have a constant that is *added* to each consecutive term. **Geometric sequences** have a number that is *multiplied* to each consecutive term. In geometric sequences, this constant term is called the **common ratio**.

Let's take our cheerleader cheer and make it a geometric sequence. If the first term is 2 and the common ratio is 2, then the cheer starts off the same, because $2 + 2 = 4$ and $(2)(2) = 4$. After that, things go upward fast.

$$2, 4, 8, 16, 32, 64, 128, 256, 512, 1024, \ldots$$

A geometric sequence can also include negative numbers. When the common ratio is a negative number (for example, –5), the sequence contains both negative and positive numbers, as in the following example:

$$1, -5, 25, -125, \ldots$$

Other, Less Pleasant Sequences

Arithmetic and geometric sequences have terms marching in lockstep, with each term affected in the same way. This is not true of every sequence you might encounter on the SAT. Some have no constant difference between the terms, or the difference between the terms keeps changing.

Here is an example of one such sequence:

$$2, 3, 6, 18, 108, 1944, \ldots$$

If you cannot immediately determine whether a sequence is arithmetic or geometric, try to find the relationship between numbers. This takes some guesswork, and there's no magic feather to help guide you. The SAT tests your ability to go the extra mile by using logic. In the above sequence, each term is the product of the two previous terms:

$$2 \times 3 = 6, 3 \times 6 = 18, 6 \times 18 = 108, 18 \times 108 = 1944, \ldots$$

You can expect to find unusual, hard-to-determine sequences hanging out in the latter part of a Math section. On easier items, a sequence most likely is either arithmetic or geometric.

SETS

A **set** is the mathematical name given to a group of items that share some common property. All positive numbers make up one set, and all prime numbers make up another. Each item in a set is called an **element** or a **member**.

Don't confuse a set with a sequence. A set is simply a collection of elements that are not necessarily related to one another, as they are in a sequence.

The **union** of two sets is another set that contains all the elements of each set. If set A contains all the blue-eyed women and set B contains all the blue-eyed men, the union of sets A and B is all blue-eyed women and men. If set A = (1, 2, 4, 6, 8) and set B = (2, 3, 5, 7, 8), the union of A and B is (1, 2, 2, 3, 4, 5, 6, 7, 8, 8).

The **intersection** of two sets is another set that contains all the elements the two sets have in common. If set A = (1, 2, 4, 6, 8) and set B = (2, 3, 5, 7, 8), the intersection of A and B is the set (2, 8).

A difficult set item involves a group of people, some of whom are engaged in activity A and others in activity B, while still others refrain from participating in either activity. Here's an example:

7. In a group of students, 24 are considered to be good at math, 14 are good at liberal arts, and 12 are good at both. How many students are in the group?

    (A)   14
    (B)   24
    (C)   26
    (D)   38
    (E)   50

To solve this item, use the following simple formula:

Total in a set = number in set 1 + number in set 2 −
intersection of set 1 and set 2 + number in neither set

You have to figure out which members belong to set 1, which to set 2, what the intersection of two sets is, and how many abstain from participating.

Total students = those in math (24) + those in liberal arts (14) −
those in both (12) + those in neither (0) = 26.

There are a total of 26 students, choice **C**.

Some set items may not explicitly tell you how many people are in neither set. If an item says that each student in a class has to learn either French or Italian, then the "neither set" (those learning neither French nor Italian) is zero.

That covers the numbers & operations basics. Now let's apply these concepts to some SAT strategies.

ESSENTIAL STRATEGIES

Before we dive into the step methods and strategies you'll use on the SAT math section, let's take a look at the types of numbers & operations items you'll encounter on the SAT.

TYPES OF ITEMS

On the new SAT, numbers & operations items are one of four basic types:

- Math Head
- Supermath Head
- Numbers Game
- The Real World

Here's a brief description of each type:

Math Head

With these items, you have to demonstrate your ability to deal with numbers and apply your knowledge of the order of operations. Solving these items simply requires knowing the fundamentals of numbers & operations, which were provided in the previous section.

3. If $5(3-8)^2 + 5(4+6) = 5x$, what is the value of x?

(A) $2^2 + 5$
(B) $5^2 + 10$
(C) $10^2 + 2$
(D) 5^3
(E) 10^3

In this example, all the information is there in the stem, and all you need to do is solve for x. However, SAT writers try to make Math Head items more convoluted by misleading you through sets of parentheses, complicated numbers, and puzzling answer choices. Luckily, you've just learned all the key concepts that SAT numbers & operations tests, so you should have no problem with these items.

Supermath Head

Think of these items as requiring several complex number operations. They're like Math Head items on steroids. Supermath Head items do their darnedest to test your knowledge of formulas and concepts, especially some of the lesser known ones. But you'll do just fine if you study and practice the essential concepts presented in this book. Here's an example:

18. 1024 is divisible by 2^n. What is the greatest possible value for n?

   (A)   6
   (B)   7
   (C)   8
   (D)   9
   (E)   10

Numbers Game

Numbers Game items test your understanding of pure numbers operations. These items cover the properties of positive, negative, even, odd, and prime numbers. Check this out:

7. If n and r are positive integers and $(n + r) \times n$ is even, which of the following MUST be false?

   (A)   If n is odd, then r is odd.
   (B)   If n is odd, then r is even.
   (C)   If n is even, then r is even.
   (D)   If n is even, then r is odd.
   (E)   If n is zero, r must be even.

The Real World

These items create real-world scenarios to test your knowledge of numbers & operations. You have to find ratios, percents, and numbers of people in sets. To solve these items, you have to translate the real-life scenario into an equation or an expression, as in this sample item:

7. Experts say that of 300 mushrooms, 25% are poisonous, and of all poisonous mushrooms, 80% are fatal. How many mushrooms are fatally poisonous?

(A) 80
(B) 75
(C) 60
(D) 100
(E) 275

EFFECTIVE STRATEGIZING

Knowing about a strategy doesn't help you if you never use it on the SAT. Many students read a book like this, say "Yes! That's all true!" then never once apply the techniques on real or practice tests. As you might expect, their scores don't improve very much, if at all.

To prevent this from happening to you, look at every item you encounter and always first ask yourself the question, "Which strategy would work well on this item?" Sometimes more than one strategy will do the trick—that's why learning many different strategies is so helpful.

The items themselves often contain clues within the stem, and that will give you a good idea of what strategy to use:

If you see	Then you probably have a . . .
Fractions, roots, radicals, or exponents that need to be added, subtracted, multiplied, or divided using fairly simple operations.	Math Head
More complex items that require using numerous operations to simplify an expression before solving it.	Supermath Head
Items that test the properties of positive, negative, even, odd, and prime numbers.	Numbers Game
Items that use a real-life context to test your knowledge of percents, sets, and ratios.	The Real World

TACKLING MATH AND SUPERMATH HEAD ITEMS

Math Head items are pretty simple, but it's easy to fall into traps if you're not careful when solving these items. The goal is to protect yourself against traps by following our four-step method. Supermath Head items are a bit more complicated, but you can use the same step method to solve these items. The only major difference between the two is that steps 2 and 3 are more intensive for Supermath Head items and may contain several different concepts and formulas.

Follow these four steps every time you approach a Math Head or Supermath Head item:

Step 1: Determine what the item is really asking you to solve.

Step 2: Determine which formulas and concepts to use.

Step 3: Do the math by writing out every step.

Step 4: Plug it in.

Math Head and Supermath Head Items in Slow Motion

Now let's work out each step in slow motion. We'll start out with a basic Math Head item:

3. If $5(3 - 8)^2 + 5(4 + 6) = 5x$, what is the value of x?

(A) $2^2 + 5$
(B) $5^2 + 10$
(C) $10^2 + 2$
(D) 5^3
(E) 10^3

Step 1: Determine what the item is really asking you to solve.

Carefully analyze the item. In this case, the ultimate goal is to find the value of x. Also notice that all the answers involve exponents.

Step 2: Determine which formulas and concepts to use.

To calculate the value of x, you first need to simplify the equation by getting rid of the parentheses and exponents so you can arrive at the answer.

To simplify the equation, you need to follow PEMDAS on the left side of the equation.

Step 3: Do the math by writing out every step.

Make sure you take the time to write out your steps. If you try doing the math in your head, you run the risk of making a careless mistake. Furthermore, writing out your work reinforces the concepts you've already learned. The more explicit you make these concepts, the easier it will be to remember them.

$$5(3-8)^2 + 5(4+6) = 5x$$

First, solve the parentheses:

$$5(-5)^2 + 5(10) = 5x$$

Now do the exponents:

$$5 \times 25 + 5(10) = 5x$$

Be very careful with signs changes depending on the odd or even exponent. Then do the multiplication:

$$125 + 50 = 5x$$

There is no division, so do the addition:

$$175 = 5x$$

Now do a little algebra and divide both sides by 5:

$$x = 35$$

Step 4: Plug it in.

Congratulations. You solved for x. Before giving your humble acceptance speech, look down at the answer choices. There's no 35, so there's one more step to go. Simplify each answer choice to see which one gives you 35.

Choice **A**:

$$2^2 + 5 = 4 + 5 = 9$$

Choice **B**:

$$5^2 + 10 = 25 + 10 = 35$$

Voilà! Answer **B** is correct.

Guided Practice

Try solving this Math Head item on your own:

6. If $5^x = 25^3$, what is the value of $(\sqrt[3]{2})^x$?

(A) $\sqrt{16}$

(B) $\sqrt{2^3}$

(C) $\sqrt{2^6}$

(D) $2^{\frac{6}{2}}$

(E) 2^4

Step 1: Determine what the item is really asking you to solve.

What is the stem asking you for? What concepts apply?

Step 2: Determine which formulas and concepts to use.

What steps do you have to follow? How can you simplify the equations?

Step 3: Do the math by writing out every step.

Be careful when you bring the numbers to the same base, and be attentive when you change the exponents.

Step 4: Plug it in.

Is the answer that you found in the form the item requires? If so, choose the correct answer. If not, what are you going to do about it?

Guided practice: Explanation

Step 1: Determine what the item is really asking you to solve.

The stem tells you that you have to figure out the value of $(\sqrt[3]{2})^x$. However, your real goal is to find the value of x. The item revolves around that unknown variable. Once you know x, you'll be able to find $(\sqrt[3]{2})^x$.

Step 2: Determine which formulas and concepts to use.

Think back to what you learned about exponents and roots in the previous section. To solve for x in the first equation, you want to simplify the numbers so that you have the same bases on either side of the equation. Once the bases are the same on both sides, the exponents will be equal. After you find the value of x, you can plug it into $(\sqrt[3]{2})^x$. To make it easier to find the answer, you might have to change $(\sqrt[3]{2})^x$ into exponential form.

Step 3: Do the math by writing out every step.

To solve $5^x = 25^3$, you need to bring both expressions to the same base. In this case, convert both bases to 5:

$$5^x = 25^3$$
$$5^x = (5^2)^3$$

Now you can solve for x:

$$5^x = (5^2)^3$$
$$5^x = 5^6$$
$$x = 6$$

Once you find x, plug it into the second expression:

$$(\sqrt[3]{2})^x = (\sqrt[3]{2})^6 = 2^{\frac{6}{3}} = 2^2 = 4$$

Step 4: Plug it in.

Now you have the answer, 4. But the stem doesn't have a plain old 4 as an answer choice. Typical. Take a close look at the choices. Answer choice **A** works out to the value you need.

Independent Practice

Here's a tougher Supermath Head item for you to solve on your own. Once you've completed your work, look at the following page to see how we solved it.

9. If $a^4 > a^5$, what is one possible value of a?

Independent Practice: Explanation

Step 1: Determine what the item is really asking you to solve.

There are no answer choices here, so this is a grid-in. The stem asks you to find out when a^4 will be greater than a^5. You need to find a number whose value *increases* when the exponent *decreases*.

Step 2: Determine which formulas and concepts to use.

How do you solve such an item? Think back to what you've learned about fractions. When fractions are multiplied by themselves, their value decreases. So a fraction raised to a higher power is less than a fraction raised to a lower power. Of course, we are talking about only positive numbers here because you can't grid in a negative number.

Step 3: Do the math by writing out every step.

Because the stem asks for one *possible* value of x, you know there's going to be more than one correct answer. Plug in an easy fraction, such as $\frac{1}{2}$, and check it:

$$\left(\frac{1}{2}\right)^4 > \left(\frac{1}{2}\right)^5$$

$$\frac{1}{16} > \frac{1}{32}$$

That works.

Step 4: Plug it in.

There is more than one correct answer to this grid-in item, but $\frac{1}{2}$ works just fine. Make sure the answer is a decimal or a proper fraction.

TACKLING NUMBERS GAME ITEMS

As you'll see, our step method is almost identical to Math and Supermath Heads. Follow these steps every time you see a Numbers Game item:

Step 1: Determine what the item is really asking you to solve.

Step 2: Determine which formulas and concepts to use.

Step 3: Do the math by writing out every step.

Step 4: Plug in numbers for variables to check your math.

Numbers Game Items in Slow Motion

We'll look at this first Numbers Game item together:

7. If n and r are positive integers and $(n + r) \times n$ is even, which of the following MUST be false?

(A)   If n is odd, then r is odd.
(B)   If n is odd, then r is even.
(C)   If n is even, then r is even.
(D)   If n is even, then r is odd.
(E)   If n is zero, r must be even.

Step 1: Determine what the item is really asking you to solve.

The stem here wants you to apply your knowledge of odd/even number operations. What it really wants you to do is to discover which n and r combination makes the product *odd*, not even.

Step 2: Determine which formulas and concepts to use.

To solve this item, you should apply the formulas you just learned in the Essential Concepts section.

Remember the multiplication table for odd/even numbers? Here it is:

$$\text{even} \times \text{even} = \text{even}$$

$$\text{even} \times \text{odd} = \text{even}$$

$$\text{odd} \times \text{odd} = \text{odd}$$

How about the addition table:

$$even + even - even$$

$$odd + odd - even$$

$$even + odd = odd$$

You definitely need to use these tables, so it is worth writing them down before you move ahead.

Step 3: Do the math by writing out every step.

From the multiplication table, you know that odd $\times$ odd = odd. So both n and $(n + r)$ should be odd.

To make the sum of $n + r$ odd, either n or r must be odd. From our multiplication chart, we know that if $n + r$ is odd, n must also be odd if we want the product of the two to be odd. Therefore, r should be even. Now go back to the answer choices. Answer **B** says that n is odd and r is even. This combination turns the answer into an odd number. Pick this answer choice.

Step 4: Plug in numbers for variables to check your math.

Now check your result with real numbers. If you don't know the formulas or don't trust your memory, you can always use real numbers to try out every answer offered or check the operations you performed.

Try out answer choice **A**: substitute n and r for odd numbers:

$$(3 + 5) \times 3 = 24$$

The answer is even and therefore should be eliminated.

Choice **B**: $(3 + 2) \times 3 = 15$

The answer is odd, which contradicts the original condition. Choice **B** gets to hang around.

Choice **C**: $(2 + 2) \times 2 = 8$

The answer is even and should be eliminated.

Plug in numbers for choices **D** and **E**, and you find out that answer **B** is the only combination that results in an odd number.

Guided Practice

Try this one on your own.

3. If $abc = d$ and the value of $a = 0$, which of the following must be true?

(A) $b = 0$
(B) $d = 0$
(C) $cb = 1$
(D) $b = 1$
(E) $d = 1$

Step 1: Determine what the item is really asking you to solve.

What do you need to solve for to determine which of the answer choices is true?

Step 2: Determine which formulas and concepts to use.

You've got a zero here: what concepts can you use to figure this item out?

Step 3: Do the math by writing out every step.

Make sure you are using the concepts and formulas appropriately. Be careful not to mix different concepts together.

Step 4: Plug in numbers for variables to check your math.

Substitute real numbers into the answer choices to ensure you did everything right.

Guided Practice: Explanation

Step 1: Determine what the item is really asking you to solve.

In this item, we are dealing with a multiplication expression in which one of the numbers equals zero.

Step 2: Determine which formulas and concepts to use.

To verify/eliminate answer choices, you have to apply the rules of multiplication by zero. Specifically, the product of zero and a number is zero:

$$0 \times n = 0$$

Step 3: Do the math by writing out every step.

Because a is zero, no matter what b and c are, the product d is always zero:

$$(0)bc = d$$

$$(0)bc = 0$$

Answer choice **B** is correct.

Step 4: Plug in numbers for variables to check your math.

Just to make sure there is only one possible answer to this item, check the equation with real numbers. Remember, the item asks you to choose the answer that *must* be true.

Check answer **A**: if $abc = d$ and a is zero, b can equal zero. But because $a = 0$, b can be any number, because the product of a and b is zero anyway. Therefore, this answer is not necessarily true.

We already know answer choice **B** works.

Check answer **C**: if $abc = d$ and a is zero, cb can equal 1. But because $a = 0$, the product of c and b can be any number, because the product of a, b, c is zero anyway. Therefore, this answer is not necessarily true.

You can work through answer choices **D** and **E** and find out that **B** is the only answer that *must* be true.

Independent Practice
Flip the page once you solve this item on your own.

7. If a is a multiple of 5, b is a multiple of 7, and $ab = c$, what is one possible value of c?

(A)   25
(B)   77
(C)   75
(D)   175
(E)   200

Independent Practice: Explanation

Step 1: Determine what the item is really asking you to solve.

You need to determine a value for c, given that a is a multiple of 5 and b is a multiple of 7.

Step 2: Determine which formulas and concepts to use.

This item is about multiples and factors. If 5 and 7 are factors of a and b, they both have to be factors of c.

Step 3: Do the math by writing out every step.

The simplest way to approach this item is to find the LCM shared by 5 and 7. Multiply the two numbers:

$$5 \times 7 = 35$$

Can you reduce 35 to a smaller number that is divisible by both 5 and 7? Nope, so the correct answer must be divisible by 35.

Step 4: Plug in numbers for variables to check your math.

Try dividing each answer choice by 35. If you do your math carefully, you find that 175, choice **D**, is the correct answer.

TACKLING THE REAL WORLD ITEMS

One last step method to learn:

Step 1: Determine what the item is really asking you to solve.

Step 2: Create an equation.

Step 3: Solve the equation.

The Real World Items in Slow Motion

All together now:

7. Experts say that of 300 mushrooms, 25% are poisonous, and of all poisonous mushrooms, 80% are fatal. How many mushrooms are fatally poisonous?

(A) 80
(B) 75
(C) 60
(D) 100
(E) 275

Step 1: Determine what the item is really asking you to solve.

The item wants you to compare parts of a whole, so you need to set up a proportion. This item is about double percents, so you need to apply your knowledge of this concept. Be careful when taking the percent of the second value.

Step 2: Create an equation.

First you need to find out how many mushrooms are poisonous, which means taking 25% of 300. Then you need to determine what 80% of the *poisonous* mushrooms is, not the total number of mushrooms. So really, you are dealing with two equations here:

$$25\% \text{ of } 300 = \text{poisonous mushrooms}$$

$$80\% \text{ of poisonous mushrooms} = \text{fatally poisonous mushrooms}$$

You can also write out the order of operations if it helps you. If you sketch out a plan, the task becomes much easier.

Step 3: Solve the equation.

Set up a proportion to find 25% of 300:

$$(25\%)(300) =$$

$$(0.25)(300) = 75$$

You have 75 poisonous mushrooms.
Now take 80% of 75:

$$(80\%)(75) =$$

$$(0.80)(75) = 60$$

So of 75 poisonous mushrooms, 60 are fatal. Answer choice **C** is correct.

Guided Practice

Try this one on your own:

5. There are 48 cars in a parking lot. One-third of them are blue, 24 are red, and the rest are white. What is the ratio of white cars to blue cars?

    (A)   1:2
    (B)   1:3
    (C)   1:6
    (D)   2:3
    (E)   5:6

Step 1: Determine what the item is really asking you to solve.

What do you have to find first to solve this item? What do you need to find the ratio? Do you have all the numbers?

Step 2: Create an equation.

Do you know the total number of each color? How can you find the missing numbers? Do you have to find the ratios of all the cars or just of white to blue?

Step 3: Solve the equation.

Be careful with your numbers. How do you find one-third of the whole? What is the whole in this item?

Guided Practice: Explanation

Step 1: Determine what the item is really asking you to solve.

The item ultimately asks you to find the ratio of white cars to blue cars. That means that you should figure out the actual numbers of cars, then compare them to each other.

Step 2: Create an equation.

In this case, you need to find out how many white, red, and blue cars there are in the parking lot. First you need to find the number of blue cars:

$$\text{blue} = \frac{1}{3}(48)$$

Then find the number of white cars:

$$\text{white} = 48 - (\text{blue} + \text{red})$$

Then you can determine the ratio of white cars to blue cars.

Step 3: Solve the equation.

First, find one-third of 48, which gives you the number of blue cars:

$$\text{blue} = \frac{1}{3}(48) = 16$$

Then find the number of white cars:

$$\text{white} = 48 - (\text{blue} + \text{red})$$

$$\text{white} = 48 - (16 + 24) = 8$$

Now find the ratio of white cars to blue cars:

$$8 \text{ white} : 16 \text{ blue}$$

$$8:16$$

You can further reduce these numbers by 8. The ratio is then 1:2, choice **A**.

Independent Practice

Turn the page after you solve this item to see our solution.

12. A medical research group is testing a new antibiotic on a random sample of patients. In this sample, 25 patients have some type of food allergies, 15 have lactose intolerance, 8 have both food allergies and lactose intolerance, and 3 have neither. What is the total number of patients in the sample?

Independent Practice: Explanation

Step 1: Determine what the item is really asking you to solve.

This grid-in item asks you to find the total number of patients in a sample that includes two sets: patients with allergies and patients with lactose intolerance. Remember that you also have patients who have both allergies and lactose intolerance, and those who have neither.

Step 2: Create an equation.

To solve this item, recall the formula for the total number of elements, which we introduced in the Essential Concepts section:

Total number = number in set 1 + number in set 2 – intersection of sets 1 and 2 + number in neither set

Total number = patients with food allergies + patients with lactose intolerance – patients with both food allergies and lactose intolerance + healthy patients

Step 3: Solve the equation.

You know the number of patients in set 1 (25) and in set 2 (15). The intersection of the two sets is 8 patients. Don't forget to add 3 healthy patients as neither.

Total number of patients = 25 + 15 – 8 + 3 = 35. Grid in this number.

TEST-TAKING STRATEGIES

In addition to all the numbers & operations concepts and step methods you have learned, you must also arm yourself with some broad SAT test-taking strategies. If you don't have the correct overall approach to the SAT, all the work you've done will fall to the wayside.

So let's start at a party. Imagine your friends have invited you to a cool house party. Hundreds of people are going to be there, and the party promises to be great fun—legal fun, of course. You had to work that day, so you arrive at the party several hours after it started.

When you walk into the house, do you search for your friends first, or do you pick out the scariest-looking person and start talking to him? Unless you like being snubbed, odds are you go through the house the first time looking for friends and other people you know. On a second pass, you might chat with some strangers, but because this is sometimes awkward, you don't usually jump into meeting them at the start.

PACING

Approach every SAT Math section like this party. On the first go-around, look at and answer the easy, familiar items first. This process is made simpler by the fact that every Math section is set up in order of difficulty. The first item is the easiest, the next item's a tiny bit tougher, and so on until the end. A typical twenty-item Math set breaks down the following way:

Difficulty	Item Number
Easy	1–6
Medium	7–14
Hard	15–20

Keep this chart in mind as you take practice tests, but also remember that the order of difficulty is simply based on what the test-makers consider to be easy, medium, and hard. You are your own person, and you may find item 15 to be much easier to complete than item 5.

Answering every item in order—no matter how long it takes—is a classic SAT mistake. Students start with item 1 and then just chug along until time is called. Don't be that chugger! If an item takes more than a minute to solve, skip it and move on to the next one. The goal on the first run through of an SAT Math section is to answer the items with which you're most comfortable. Save the other items for the second go-around. Although the next item is statistically a little tougher, you might find it easier to answer.

THE SAT IS NOT A NASCAR-SANCTIONED EVENT

The SAT is a timed test, and some people take this to mean that they should answer items as quickly as possible. They cut corners on items to speed through a section. This is a classic error, and an especially disastrous policy on SAT Math since the "easiest" items are at the beginning. If the last item had a fifty-point bonus attached to it, things would be different, but every item counts the same. Getting two hard items right won't do you any good if you miss two easy items in your haste. You'll be better off answering the easy items correctly, and then using whatever time you have left to take an educated guess on the remaining harder items.

Accuracy counts more than speed. First, go through a section and answer all the items that come easily to you. Then:

- Take the time to answer every one of these items *correctly*.
- Take another shot at the remaining items during the second run-through. If you spend two minutes, and the item still doesn't yield an answer, take a guess and move on.

To achieve the second point, avoid choosing the answer that looks "right" at first glance. On easy items, this choice may well be the correct answer. For items numbered 12 or higher, an answer that screams "Ooh! Ooh! Pick me and hurry on!" should be handled like a live snake. SAT distractors are designed to catch the eye of students in a hurry. More often than not, an answer choice for a hard item that looks too good to be true is exactly that: *too good to be true*.

Remember, if you can safely eliminate one of the answer choices as being wrong, you should take a guess because you may beat the wrong-answer penalty.

For most students, the best method for picking up points in the Math section is by:

- Answering all the easy items correctly
- Slowing down and catching most of the medium items
- Getting 25 to 50 percent of the hard items right

This approach is not as thrilling as getting the hardest five items right (while chancing tons of mistakes along the way), but it does put you on the best path to a high score.

WEAR YOUR NO. 2 DOWN TO A NUB

There are many students who are afraid of placing a smudge on their test booklets. These students don't write down any formulas or equations. They don't write out their work when manipulating numbers. They don't score very well on the SAT either.

Get over your respect for the SAT test booklet. Write all over those rough, recycled pages. When you are finished, your test booklet should be covered with scrawls, notes, computations, and drawings. In fact, the simple act of writing something down for every item helps improve your SAT score. It forces you to put your thoughts down on paper instead of trying to solve items in your head. If you try to answer items in your head, the SAT will chew you up and spit you out.

Be a smart test-taker. Jot down everything you can.

TAKE A DEEP BREATH AND . . .

Don't freak out when you take the SAT. Sure, the test is important, but many people act as though their entire lives depend on how they do on this one exam. It's not true! It's just one test, and you can even take it over again.

On test day, you want to sit down feeling confident and positive. Do what you have to do to get into that mindset—wear a lucky bracelet, do a hundred push-ups, write love poetry—because you need to believe in yourself when taking the SAT. A positive outlook increases your willingness to take an educated guess on a tough numbers & operations item instead of leaving it blank. It helps you trust your inner ear, enabling you to answer a grammar item, even though you don't know the exact grammatical rule being tested. A positive approach to the SAT is more important than any single fact or strategy you could learn. Banish anxiety from your mind, and all the skills and strategies you've learned to prepare for the SAT will take its place.

THE 8 MOST COMMON MISTAKES

As you prepare, keep the following common mistakes in mind. Some are mistakes to avoid when taking the actual test. Others are mistakes to avoid during your preparation for the test.

1. Forgetting one of the essential numbers & operations concepts. Know your terms and concepts cold.
2. Trying to manipulate an equation in your head instead of writing it down and solving it.
3. Not solving for what the item actually asks.
4. Failing to work through the practice sets in this book—*reading* the book is not enough!
5. Failing to practice the step methods on every practice test item. You need these methods when the answer isn't obvious to you.
6. Refusing to guess after eliminating one answer choice.
7. Answering every item in order.
8. Rushing through a set instead of thinking each item through.

CONCLUSION

Without practice, you won't master SAT numbers & operations. You've learned quite a bit since you picked up this little book, but now comes the hard part—*you* have to apply it to testlike items. There are two practice sets at the end of this book: one made up of multiple-choice items and one made up of grid-ins. Here are some tips for getting the most out of these items.

- **Do not time yourself on the first practice set**. When you begin, don't worry about time at all. Take as long as you need to work through each set.

- **Read the explanations for all items, regardless of whether you got them right or wrong**. This is critical—always read *all* the explanations for each set's items. The idea is to develop skills that help you score points as quickly as possible. Most important, scoring a point doesn't mean you got it in the most efficient manner. The overarching goal is to *apply* the methods you've learned. Whether you get all, some, or none of the practice items right doesn't matter.

After the first set, you may want to start paying attention to time. Certainly by the actual test, give yourself about a minute or so per item.

All the vital information and snazzy strategies you learn in this book won't do a lick of good if you don't use them on the day of the test. Sadly, this happens more often than you might think. Students acquire useful tips, but once the test starts on Saturday morning, all of it goes out the window.

To help ensure this doesn't happen to your, tackle these sets *using the skills and strategies you have just learned*. Don't worry about how many you get right or wrong; they're just practice sets. Instead, focus on how well you use the techniques you've learned. When you look at a numbers & operations item, can you tell what method would work best? If it's a Real World item, how do you translate the information into an equation? If it's a Numbers Game item, what are some good numbers to use as substitutes for the variables?

Don't get frustrated by your progress on the practice sets. Every mistake you make on the practice sets is one that you will avoid on the real test. Yes, there are some rules you don't know, but learning about these on practice items corrects that deficit. When the real SAT rolls around, you'll have yet another tool in your arsenal that you can employ if needed.

ADDITIONAL ONLINE PRACTICE

Once you're done working through the items and explanations in this book, you can practice further by going online to **testprep.sparknotes.com** and taking full-length SAT tests. These practice tests provide you with instant feedback, delineating all your strengths and weaknesses.

Also, be sure to take the free numbers & operations posttest to see how well you've absorbed the content of this book. For this posttest, go to **testprep.sparknotes.com/powertactics**.

FINALLY . . .

The goal of this book is to show you effective methods for answering SAT numbers & operations items. We hope this helps strip away some of the mystery about the SAT that causes so many students to freak out on test day. You should realize that the SAT is not a perfect indicator of your math ability. In fact, it simply tests your knowledge on a narrow range of math topics. Master those topics, and you will conquer the SAT.

On to the practice items!

THE PRACTICE
SETS

SET 1: MULTIPLE CHOICE

1. The number 48 consists of how many distinct prime factors?

   (A) 1
   (B) 2
   (C) 3
   (D) 4
   (E) 5

2. Which of the following fractions is in its simplest reduced form?

   (A) $\frac{17}{136}$

   (B) $\frac{7}{126}$

   (C) $\frac{13}{69}$

   (D) $\frac{11}{121}$

   (E) $\frac{5}{160}$

3. The number 210 is divisible by all of the following integers EXCEPT

   (A) 6
   (B) 8
   (C) 10
   (D) 21
   (E) 35

4. In the arithmetic sequence $(5, 9, 13, 17, \ldots)$, where $n_1 = 5$, what is the value of n_8?

   (A) 29
   (B) 33
   (C) 37
   (D) 41
   (E) 45

5. If $2(5 \quad 8)^2 \quad \text{I} \quad 3(6 \text{ I } 2) = 7x$, what is the value of x?

    (A) $2^2 + 1$
    (B) $3^2 - 3$
    (C) $2^2 + 3$
    (D) 2^3
    (E) 3^2

6. A master of the secretarial arts types at a rate of 55 words per minute. If there are 330 words per page, how many pages could a master be expected to type in four and a half hours?

    (A) 6
    (B) 12
    (C) 37.5
    (D) 45
    (E) 247.5

$$
\begin{array}{r}
3X \\
X6 \\
+ XX \\
\hline
12X
\end{array}
$$

7. In the correctly worked addition problem above, which digit could represent X?

    (A) 2
    (B) 4
    (C) 6
    (D) 8
    (E) 0

8. If b is a positive integer, which of the following equals $3b^4$?

    (A) $\sqrt{81b^{56}}$

    (B) $\sqrt{9b^8}$

    (C) $\sqrt{9b^{16}}$

    (D) $9\sqrt{b^{16}}$

    (E) $b^3\sqrt{9b^2}$

9. If set S consists of all positive prime integers greater than 5 and set T consists of all positive odd integers less than 21, which of the following must be true?

    I.   Set T contains more numbers than set S.
    II. There are no even numbers in either set S or set T.
    III. All numbers in set S are in set T.

    (A) I
    (B) II
    (C) I and III
    (D) II and III
    (E) I, II, III

10. In the geometric sequence $(4, 12, 36, 108, 324, \ldots)$, where $n_1 = 4$, what is the value of n_9?

    (A) $(2^2)(3^8)$
    (B) $(2^2)(3^9)$
    (C) 2^{36}
    (D) 6^9
    (E) $(2^9)(3^8)$

11. When s is divided by 6, the remainder is 5. What is the remainder when $2s$ is divided by 6?

    (A) 1
    (B) 2
    (C) 3
    (D) 4
    (E) 5

12. 288 is divisible by 2^n. What is the greatest possible value for n?

    (A) 5
    (B) 6
    (C) 7
    (D) 8
    (E) 9

13. z is a multiple of 3, and y is a multiple of 5. a is an even integer divisible by both z and y. Therefore, a could equal which of the following?

    (A) 45
    (B) 62
    (C) 75
    (D) 80
    (E) 90

14. If $-1 < x < 0$, then which of the following MUST be true?

    (A) $x^2 < x^3 < x$
    (B) $x < x^2 < x^3$
    (C) $x^3 < x^2 < x$
    (D) $x^3 < x < x^2$
    (E) $x < x^3 < x^2$

15. When 8^{263} is expanded out, what digit will be in the units (1's) space?

    (A) 8
    (B) 4
    (C) 2
    (D) 6
    (E) 5

16. There are six numbers in a certain arithmetic sequence, the sum of which is 297. If the last number in the sequence is 67, by what constant amount is each number increased in the sequence?

    (A) 3
    (B) 7
    (C) 14
    (D) 30
    (E) 32

17. The first two terms of set A are 2 and 3. The rest of the terms are obtained either by adding the two previous terms together, when the last term is odd, or by subtracting the previous term from the term before it, when the last term is even. What is the mode of set A?

    (A) −3
    (B) −2
    (C) 0
    (D) 2
    (E) 3

18. If $s^m = 64$ and s and m are both integers, what is the LEAST possible value of $s - m$?

    (A) 4

    (B) −4

    (C) −6

    (D) −8

    (E) −12

19. If $4^x = 64^{12}$, what is the value of $\left(\sqrt[3]{2}\right)^x$?

    (A) 2^{36}

    (B) 2^{24}

    (C) 2^{16}

    (D) 2^{12}

    (E) 2^{6}

20. A geometric sequence consists of five terms, the sum of which is 1023. If the common ratio of the sequence is 4, what is the first term of the sequence?

    (A) −9

    (B) −6

    (C) 3

    (D) 6

    (E) 9

ANSWERS & EXPLANATIONS

1. **B**

You have the phrase "distinct prime factors," and if you have the definition of all three terms in that large Math Head of yours, you should have little difficulty with this item:

Distinct—the numbers must be different

Prime—divisible only by 1 and itself

Factor—an integer that divides into another integer evenly

Let's do the prime factorization of 48 and see what we get:

$$
\begin{aligned}
48 &= \\
6 \times 8 &= \\
2 \times 3 \times 8 &= \\
2 \times 3 \times 2 \times 2 \times 2
\end{aligned}
$$

The prime factorization of 48 gives you four 2s and a 3. There are five factors (choice **E**) in total, but the stem wanted the number of *distinct* prime factors. This cancels out all the repeated 2s, so the number of distinct prime factors is two (2 and 3). That's choice **B**.

2.   C

Talking about simple fractions seems vaguely cruel, but we promise not to make fun of the simple fraction in front of its city cousins. Simple fractions are fractions that can't be reduced any more. Four of the answer choices can be reduced. Your goal is to find the one that can't.

Take a first pass through the answer choices and see whether there are any obvious choices for further reduction. Choice **E** springs to mind, because the 5 in the numerator could easily go into the 160 in the denominator. This fraction can actually be reduced, but why? It's enough to realize that it *can* be reduced. Once you determine that, cross it out and move on.

The remaining answer choices all have prime numbers in their numerators. This is good news, because it means you only have to use your calculator and try to divide the lower number (denominator) by the upper number (numerator).

For choice **A**, you punch in 136/17 = 8. Because this is a whole number, this fraction can be reduced. Cross out choice **A** and keep chugging.

Choice **B**: 126/7 − 18. Nope.

Choice **C**: 69/13 = 5.307 something. Choice **C** can't be reduced. It's your answer.

3.   B

The wording in the stem is different, but the methods you use to solve it are exactly the same as the previous item. In item 2, we took the denominators and tested to see whether they were divisible by the numerators in order to determine whether the fraction could be reduced. On item 3, the same process is being done, only this time the number we're testing remains the same (210).

Take a moment and look at items 2 and 3. They show how math terms can be switched around to pose essentially the same question. This is why you need to know the *terms*, not just have a passing familiarity with them. Anything less than true understanding can get you in a bind on a tough item.

Luckily, this isn't a tough item: you know that because it's only the third. Trusting the heavy math lifting to your calculator, we can start with choice **A** and see that it divides into 210 evenly:

Choice **A**: 210/6 = 35. You can look down and cross out both choices **A** and **E** with this information.

Choice **B**: 210/8 = 26.25. Nothing clean about that .25. Choice **B** is your nondivisible culprit.

4. **B**

You can tackle sequence items by going all algebraic and setting up a nifty little formula to solve them. Although this method would certainly impress the members of your school's Variable Lovers Club, it's not the smartest path on the SAT. The main reason it's a bad idea is that all the distractors are set up to trap students who do all the math. You play right into the SAT's hands by tackling an item in this manner. This doesn't mean you won't get it right. It just means you run a much greater risk of getting it wrong, because the incorrect answer choices are all designed to catch people who make a mistake working the algebra.

So go low-tech instead. *Write stuff out.* You should write work down on every item, every time, and solve the items on paper, not in your head. For this sequence item, take 15 seconds to write out:

$n1$	$n2$	$n3$	$n4$	$n5$	$n6$	$n7$	$n8$

Now place the numbers given to you in the stem underneath:

$n1$	$n2$	$n3$	$n4$	$n5$	$n6$	$n7$	$n8$
5	9	13	17				

As you can see, 4 is added to each number in the sequence. Finish up the list and you have your answer. Furthermore, you know it's right *and* you can come back and check your work very easily if you have the time at the end of the section. Those last two points are just as important as the first one.

$n1$	$n2$	$n3$	$n4$	$n5$	$n6$	$n7$	$n8$
5	9	13	17	21	25	29	33

Choice **B** is 33.

5.   B

Before jumping into PEMDAS, take a look at the answer choices. None of them are actual integers. They all have some arithmetic work that needs to be done before they can be determined. Sometimes there's a reason for this, such as the equation can't be solved completely and has to remain in a seemingly unfinished state. This time, though, the answer choices are like this simply to bust your chops and make you use knowledge of exponents correctly.

Before we jump into the answer choices, let's solve that equation. It's all about order of operations, as discussed on pages 16–17. Start with parentheses, then exponents, then multiplication and division, and finally addition and subtraction:

$$2(5-8)^2 + 3(6+2) = 7x$$
$$2(-3)^2 + 3(8) = 7x$$
$$2(9) + 3(8) = 7x$$
$$18 + 24 = 7x$$
$$42 = 7x$$
$$6 = x$$

Where's a 6 when you need it? It's at Choice **B**, because $3^2 - 3 = 9 - 3 = 6$.

6.   D

Here's a chatty little item with all sorts of embedded facts:

How fast a master types: 55 words/minute

Number of words on a page: 330 words

Number of hours of typing: 4.5 hours

The main thing working to your advantage on this item is that it is item 6. This makes it an easy item. If it were item 20, you could expect none of the numbers to divide evenly, and all sorts of horrid improper fractions would need to be carried from one part to the next to solve it.

We'll get to some nasty items later. For now, though, let's get some points where the getting is good. If a master types at 55 words/minute and there are 330 words/page, then the amount of time it would take to type one page is:

$$\frac{330 \text{ words/page}}{55 \text{ words/minute}} = 6 \text{ minutes for each page}$$

In an hour, then, a master of the secretarial arts could type 10 pages, because

$$\frac{60 \text{ minutes/hour}}{6 \text{ minutes/page}} = 10 \text{ pages/hour}$$

With 4.5 hours to type, the typist could complete:

$$(10 \text{ pages/hour})(4.5 \text{ hours}) = 45 \text{ pages}$$

That's choice **D**.

7.   B

There might be a way to solve this algebraically, but why bother? The answer is literally right in front of you. Granted, there are four wrong answer choices clouding up the issue, but instead of racking your brain and coming up with the right solution, just hit the answer choices and start seeing which ones work and which don't.

The best place to start is along the right side of the equation. You have $X + 6 + X = X$. Start plugging in answer choices to see whether they work. If they don't work there, they won't work on the left side of the item. You can cross them out immediately and not worry about the second part.

Choice **E** is a prime candidate for elimination, because $0 + 6 + 0 = 6$, not 0. (That's the units digits of the stem.) Because we've started on that end, might as well try 8 next:

$$X + 6 + X = 6$$

$8 + 6 + 8 = 22$, not 28. A 2 is not an 8, no matter what a politician might say. **D** is out.

Choice **C**:

$$X + 6 + X = 6$$

$$6 + 6 + 6 = 18$$

No 6 at the end here, either.

Choice **B**:

$$X + 6 + X = 6$$

$$4 + 6 + 4 = 14$$

Bingo. This works here. Let's put a 4 in the tens place and see whether it all works out.

$$
\begin{array}{r}
34 \\
46 \\
+\ 44 \\
\hline
124
\end{array}
$$

Your calculator will confirm that this is correct. **B**'s the answer. See? It was right there in front of you all the time.

8. **B**

The easy items are behind you now and you are in the Medium Item Zone. The items might not look any different, but don't let that fool you. Answers that seem very easy are probably too easy to be the right answers.

Item 8 talks a lot about the integer b, but it's easier to understand what happens to the 3 in front of the variable. If there is a 3 *outside* a square root sign, what value would it be *inside*? To put it another way, 3 is the square root of what number? The answer is 9, and this shouldn't come as some big surprise. If it does, you'll want to review the first ten perfect squares on page 32.

Because you need a 9 inside the square root sign, choices **A** and **D** are a bust. Cross them out. From here, you have at least a one-in-three chance when guessing if the b^4 stumps you. Many students gravitate toward choice **C**, because 16 is the square of 4. That's true for regular numbers, but we're looking at exponents here (tiny raised numbers and all), not regular numbers.

Let's go back to the 3 and use it as an example. You can write 3 as 3^1 if you want. Once we place it inside the square root sign, the 3 becomes a 9, or 3^2. In Mathspeak:

$$
3 = \sqrt{9}
$$
$$
3^1 = \sqrt{3^2}
$$

So the exponent doubles from 1 to 2 when it comes under the square root sign. You can expect the exponent of b^4 to double as well, becoming b^8 under the sign. The answer is choice **B**.

9. **B**

Here's a roman numeral item, and you might want to skip these items until the very end. The reason is simple: you have to do the work of three items to get credit for one. It's not the best use of your time, especially because there are other medium items not divided into three parts still to be encountered.

Having said that, let's jump in and play the Numbers Game. Set S contains all positive prime integers greater than 5, which is a huge amount of numbers. The first bunch of numbers in set S are going to be 7, 11, 13, 17, 19, and 23, but it will go on and on.

Set T is a little more constrained. We could actually write out all positive odd integers less than 21 below:

$$\text{Set } T = \{1, 3, 5, 7, 9, 11, 13, 15, 17, 19\}$$

All this work and still no payoff. Time to review the roman numerals.

Roman numeral I is wrong. Crazy wrong, because set S has an infinite number of numbers, and set T has 10. So we can go into the answer choices and cross out any choice that contains roman numeral I. This gets rid of **A**, **C**, and **E**. You have only two remaining choices, **B** "II only" and **D** "II and III only."

Think carefully about this. What roman numeral should you check next? If you said numeral III, good for you. There's nothing to be gained by checking numeral II, because you still have to check numeral III to determine the right answer. However, if you try III next, you have your answer without having to check II at all. If III works, the answer is **D**. If it doesn't, the only choice left is **B**, and that's the answer.

Roman numeral III claims, "All numbers in set S are in set T." A quick glance at the numbers in sets S and T shows you this isn't true. III is wrong, so answer choice **B** must be the right answer.

10. **A**

This item is a geometric sequence, and the numbers are larger, but you can attack it the same way you handled item 4. And why not? The low-tech approach got that item right. It can do the same on this medium item.

The stem asks for n_9 and gives you the first five values of the sequence. Jotting away, you would write down:

$n1$	$n2$	$n3$	$n4$	$n5$	$n6$	$n7$	$n8$	$n9$
4	12	36	108	324				

How are the numbers changing? It's not addition this time. It's multiplication. Each value is 3 times larger than the previous one. So type 324 into your calculator, then multiply by 3 to get the next value and the next, and so on, until you reach n_9:

$n1$	$n2$	$n3$	$n4$	$n5$	$n6$	$n7$	$n8$	$n9$
4	12	36	108	324	972	2916	8748	26,244

Without a calculator, working out these numbers takes too much time. But that's a moot point because you get to use one. Use it to fill out this sequence table, and you find 26244. Now you use your flat electronic friend to go through the answer choices. Starting with **A**, you find:

$$(2^2)(3^8) = 4 \times 6561 = 26{,}244$$

There's your answer.

11. **D**

This item requires two things:

1. You have to be enough of a Math Head to remember what a *remainder* is.
2. You need to realize that using real numbers is better than trying to solve this item algebraically.

If there is some abstract way to determine the answer, it's not worth printing here. Instead, come up with a real number that leaves a remainder of 5 whenever it's divided by 6. This is item 11, and it just so happens that when 11 is divided by 6, the dividend—there's some third-grade Mathspeak coming at you—is 1 and the remainder is 5.

So $s = 11$. That means $2s = (2)(11) = 22$. Now let's divide 22 by 6 and see what we get.

$$\begin{array}{r} 3 \text{ r}4 \\ 6\overline{)\,22} \\ -18 \\ \hline 4 \end{array}$$

You get 4 as your remainder, which is answer choice **D**. Without worrying about the abstract reasons for this, move on.

12. **A**

The number 2 is a prime number, so the best approach to this item is to make a factor tree out of 288. If you do it correctly, you have a slew of 2's at the bottom of the tree. You can then add them up to find the greatest value.

$$288$$

$$2 \times 144$$

$$2 \times 2 \times 72$$

$$2 \times 2 \times 2 \times 36$$

$$2 \times 2 \times 2 \times 2 \times 18$$

$$2 \times 2 \times 2 \times 2 \times 2 \times 9$$

$$2^5 \times 9$$

You might have taken a faster route, but the bottom of your factor tree will look the same. The greatest possible value for n is 5, choice **A**.

13. **E**

You could call this a Numbers Game item with a dose of Math Head thrown in for grins. As is often the case, the stem sounds very confusing, but if you understand the terms, you have little to worry about. If a is an even integer divisible by both z and y, then a must be a number divisible by both 3 and 5 (these are the two numbers that z and y are multiples of). The safest way to find a number that's divisible by both 3 and 5 is to multiply 3 and 5 together, then search for values divisible by this new number, 15. Anything divisible by 15 is going to be a multiple of both 3 and 5.

Answer choice **A**, 45, seems to fit the bill, because 45 = 15 × 3. Before you head on to the next item, though, take care to recall that a is an **even** integer but 45 is not even. Choice **A** is a distractor designed to catch people who play the numbers game correctly but forget the little fact that a is even. Choice **C**, 75, is another such trap. The answer is **E**, 90, because this is the only value that satisfies all the conditions for a.

14. **E**

The difficulty of this item lies in a simple fact of math: multiplying by negative fractions less than 1 is an exercise in weirdness. Most numbers get bigger when you multiply them by themselves, but not fractions less than 1. They get smaller. Add in the negative value, and you get values flipping back and forth between positive and negative, depending on whether the exponent is even or odd.

Trying to solve this item abstractly would be a poor choice, so let's give x an easy value to mess with. We say $x = -\frac{1}{2}$ and place this value into every x in the answer choices. Then it's just a matter of seeing what turns up.

For no reason other than it's there, let's start with choice **A**:

$$x^2 < x^3 < x$$

$$\left(-\frac{1}{2}\right)^2 < \left(-\frac{1}{2}\right)^2 < -\frac{1}{2}$$

$$\frac{1}{4} < -\frac{1}{8} < -\frac{1}{2}$$

Nope. Each value is wrong.

You can continue plugging away, but we can also stare at these results and see whether there's anything we can learn. We stated earlier that the value of the x term was going to flip back and forth between positive and negative, depending on the value of the exponent. You can see this in choice **A**, where the largest value is $x^2 = \frac{1}{4}$, because the exponent is even.

Think about this fact before attempting choices **B** and **C**. Each choice has x^2 as a middle value, supposedly less than the x term to the right of it that has an odd exponent. This is wrong, and you know it's wrong because a negative fraction isn't going to be larger than a positive one, regardless of what's in the numerator or denominator. You've proven that in choice **A**.

This knocks out **B** and **C** without having to do the math. It's down to **D** or **E**. You need only try one of them. If it's right, pick it. If not, choose the other. Let's try **D**:

$$x^3 < x < x^2$$

$$\left(-\frac{1}{2}\right)^3 < -\frac{1}{2} < \left(-\frac{1}{2}\right)^2$$

$$-\frac{1}{8} < -\frac{1}{2} < \frac{1}{4}$$

That's doesn't work, becuase $-\frac{1}{8}$ is greater than $-\frac{1}{2}$: remember, the

smaller a negative value is, the closer it is to zero. **E** is the correct answer.

15. C

Whoa! If you don't understand how the SAT works, this item will leave you pole-axed. If there is an abstract mathematical way to solve this item, only math wizards know it.

You should hit this item and just start writing stuff down. Again and again on the SAT, the students who are willing to place work on paper get rewarded. Figuring out what 8^{263} is would take a supercomputer, not a calculator. Why not start smaller? Figure out some simpler values of 8 and see what happens. Your calculator will do all the heavy lifting:

		Units Digit
$8^1 =$	8....................	8
$8^2 =$	64..................	4
$8^3 =$	512...............	2
$8^4 =$	4096.............	6
$8^5 =$	37268............	8
$8^6 =$	262144..........	4

Look at the units digits. It goes 8, 4, 2, 6, 8, then 4. See a pattern? Multiply 262,144 by 8, and you get a units digits of 2, because the pattern seems to be 8-4-2-6, over and over again, all the way to 8^{263} and beyond.

SET 1: MULTIPLE CHOICE

If you divide 263 by 4, you get 65 with a remainder of 3. Your chart shows you that $8^4 = 4,096$, so you would start at the 6, then go three places to the left in the pattern.

Pattern

8 4 2 6 8 4 2 6 8 4 2 6 8 4 2 6
          1 2 3

$$\frac{263}{4} = 65\ r3$$

The answer is choice **C**, 2.

16. **B**

All hard items involve multiple steps. There's no getting around that. However, some can be answered easier than others if you don't bother with the highfalutin math and consider just the answer choices given to you. Consider this sequence item. There's probably some wacky formula you can devise. Don't. Just take what the item gives you and run with it. Here's one way:

You have six numbers, and you know the last one. Each answer choice represents what the constant might be. All six numbers add up to 297. So write down:

$$\_\_\ \_\_\ \_\_\ \_\_\ \_\_\ 67 = 297$$

Let's start with choice **C**. If 14 is the constant value, then the value next to 67 will be $67 - 14 = 53$. The next value will be $53 - 14 = 39$. Use your calculator and figure out all the values. Your six numbers will look like this:

−3	11	25	39	53	67

What does this add up to? $-3 + 11 + 25 + 39 + 53 + 67 = 192$. This is not right, because it has to add up to 297 to be the right answer. The problem is that 14 is too large a number to subtract each time. If you subtract 14 from each value, you end up with six numbers that are too small. Therefore, you need a number smaller than 14.

This crosses out choices **D** and **E**. You have a 50/50 shot right now because it's either **A** or **B**. You can take a guess if time is running out, or

SAT POWER TACTICS | Numbers & Operations

81

you can try one. Let's try **B**. Starting with 67 and subtracting 7 to get the other five values, you end up with:

| 32 | 39 | 46 | 53 | 60 | 67 |

What does this add up to? $32 + 39 + 46 + 53 + 60 + 67 = 297$. There's your answer.

The goal of the SAT is to answer items correctly. Nothing more, nothing less.

17. **E**

The quicker you place pencil to paper and start writing stuff down, the faster you'll find the answer. To find the mode of set A, you need some more values. You have two to start with, 2 and 3. Following the somewhat convoluted directions, because 3 is odd, the next term is found by adding the two last terms together. $2 + 3 = 5$, so the third term is 5:

$$\text{Set } A = \{2, 3, 5\}$$

The number 5 is also odd, so the next term is $3 + 5 = 8$. The number 8 is even, so the next term is found by subtracting the term before it, $8 - 5 = 3$. Going on, set A shapes up like this:

$$\text{Set } A = \{2, 3, 5, 8, 3, 11, 14, 3, 17, 20, 3, 23, \ldots\}$$

Every third term is 3, and all other terms keep getting bigger and bigger. The mode is 3, choice **E**.

18. **D**

This is a Supermath Head item, because simple knowledge of exponents won't be enough. You have to be able to manipulate s^m to get the smallest number for $s - m$ that you can.

The first thing to do is make m as big as you can and s as small as possible. 64 is 8^2, but this can be reduced even more:

$$64 = 8^2$$
$$64 = (4 \times 2)^2$$
$$64 = (2 \times 2 \times 2)^2$$
$$64 = (2^3)^2$$
$$64 = 2^6$$

That's pretty good. You have a small $s(2)$ and a large $m(6)$, so $s - m$ would be $2 - 6 = -4$. Not bad. Not correct, either. You see, Supermath Head, because you have an even exponent (6), you can have a negative value for s, such as -2:

$$2^6 = 64 = (-2)^6$$

This gives you a value for $s - m$ that is $-2 - 6 = -8$, choice **D**. That's the lowest value possible.

19. D

To determine what $\sqrt[3]{2^x}$ is, you need to find a value for x. That's where the equation $4^x = 64^{12}$ comes in. Having a Supermath Head knowledge of exponents helps a lot on this item too.

Let's tackle the equation first. You could use your calculator and try to find the value of 64^{12}, but there's a better way to solve for x. You need to know how to manipulate exponents:

$$4^x = (64)^{12}$$
$$4^x = (4 \times 16)^{12}$$
$$4^x = (4 \times 4 \times 4)^{12}$$
$$4^x = (4^3)^{12}$$
$$4^x = 4^{36}$$

64 is the cube of 4. When you have an exponent taken to another exponent, you multiply the two numbers together, for example:

$$3 \times 12 = 36$$

This gives you a value for x of 36. When you take the cube root of a number with an exponent, you divide the exponent by 3. See what we mean about really knowing how to manipulate exponents?

$$(\sqrt[3]{2})^x = (\sqrt[3]{2})^{36} = 2^{\frac{36}{3}} = 2^{12}, \text{ choice } \mathbf{D}.$$

20. C

Last item. Whew! It's a sequence item like item 16. Like that item, you should sidestep the math and jump into the answers. It's unlikely that a sequence where five numbers are multiplied by 4 and sum to 1023 would start with a negative value, because a negative value would make the entire sum negative.

We can cross out **A** and **B**, then. Let's try choice **D**, 6, and see what happens. We'll create the five numbers exactly as the stem asks us. Take the first term, multiply by 4 to get the second term, then multiply the second term by 4 to find the third term, and so on:

6	24	96	384	1536

Does this sum to 1023? Not likely, because the last term is 1536. Because this is too large, the first term must be smaller than 6. There's only one choice, **C**, that's smaller than 6. It's the answer. Double-check if you like.

SET 2: GRID-INS

1. If the prime factors of y are 2, 5, and 11, what is one possible value for y, when $y > 500$?

2. In a certain parking lot, there are 24 blue cars, 16 red cars, and the rest are white cars. If there is a total of 48 cars in the parking lot, what is the ratio of white cars to blue cars?

3. It takes $1/3$ lb. of sausage mixed with $2/3$ lb. of beans mixed with 1 lb. of rice to make jambalaya for 6 people. How many pounds of sausage are needed to make jambalaya for 27 people?

4. Integer k is a multiple of 3 and between 100 and 150. When k is divided by 7, the remainder is 4. What is one possible value of k?

5. At Ambrose Bierce's family Thanksgiving dinner, he offered his relatives both turkey and tofurkey. At dinner, 16 relatives had turkey, and 24 had tofurkey. If 12 relatives had both turkey and tofurkey, how many relatives came to Ambrose Bierce's Thanksgiving dinner?

6. Set A consists of all even integers, and set B consists of all integers equal to or less than 1. If x is the intersection of the two sets, what is one possible value of x?

7. 500% of 30% of 36 is what percent of 216?

8. What is the least of seven consecutive integers whose sum equals 168?

9. If $x^3 > x^4$, what is one possible value of x?

10. Integers 1–49 are written out to create one number (1,234,567, 891,011,121,314,... 4,849). The number will consist of how many digits?

11. Consecutive integers 15–30 are multiplied together to produce one product. How many factors of 3 does the product contain?

12. There are 150 students in the junior class at Joseph McCarthy High School. Of them, $1/3$ bike to school, and the rest take the bus. If there are 45 boys in the class and 15 of them bike, how many girls take the bus?

13. Set R consists of a geometric sequence where the first term is 17 and the constant ratio is 6. Set S consists of an arithmetic sequence where the first term is 87 and the constant term is 175. If set T consists of all positive integers less than 1,000, what is the intersection of all three sets?

14. There are 3,600 pieces of candy divided into three different colors: red, blue, and green. There are more blue pieces than red and more green pieces than blue. If there are 1,000 red pieces, what is the LARGEST amount of blue pieces possible?

15. Delilah decides to start saving money, but she wants to start slow. On the first day, she saves 1 cent, on the second day she saves 2 cents, and on the third day she saves 4 cents. Each day she continues to save double what she saved the previous day. In dollars, how much will she have saved after 10 days?

ANSWERS & EXPLANATIONS

1.   **550**

Add up the prime factors you have and see where you are: $(2)(5)(11) =$ 110. This is less than 500, so you can't just stop here. What you can do is multiply 110 by 2, 5, or 11. It said these numbers were the prime factors, but it didn't say there was only one 2, one 5, and one 11. Multiplying 110 by another 5 gives you $(110)(5) = 550$. Grid this number in.

There are other values that would also work, such as $(110)(11) =$ 1,210. That's one of the strange things about the grid-in items. There is often more than one correct answer that you can use.

2.   **1/3**

To find the number of white cars, subtract the two values that you do know:

$$\text{Total cars} = \text{blue cars} + \text{red cars} + \text{white cars}$$

$$48 = 24 + 16 + \text{white cars}$$

$$48 = 40 + \text{white cars}$$

$$8 = \text{white cars}$$

The item wants the ratio of white cars to blue cars:

White cars/blue cars $= \dfrac{8}{24} = \dfrac{1}{3}$. Grid in this ratio.

3. **1.5**

This item also employs ratios, but it does so in a more subtle manner. The simplest way to find out how much sausage is needed for 27 people is to set up a ratio, then cross multiply:

$$\frac{1/3 \text{lb sausage}}{6 \text{ people}} = \frac{s \text{lbs sausage}}{27 \text{ people}}$$

$$\left(\frac{1}{3}\right)(27) = 6s$$

$$9 = 6s$$

$$\frac{9}{6} = s = \frac{3}{2} = 1.5$$

Remember that you can grid in either $\dfrac{3}{2}$ or 1.5, but you can't grid in the mixed fraction $1\dfrac{1}{2}$.

4. **102**

Ah, if there were multiple-choice answers below, we could jump down to them and start trying them out. This would be preferable to what we have to do, which is to actually do the math. It's one reason why multiple-choice items are easier to tackle than grid-in items—you have more options for how to solve them.

  Let's start with 99, which is the multiple of 3 just less than 100. The next multiple of 3 up from 99 is 99 + 3 = 102. If we divide 102 by 7, we get 102/7 = 14, remainder 4. Huzzah! There's one of the possible values for k that satisfies all the requirements. Grid in 102 and escape.

5. **28**

This item raises the even bigger question, "Who would actually eat tofurkey?" Setting that aside for the moment, the stem calls for you to figure out the total number of guests. To do this, add together the ones who ate turkey (16) and the ones who ate tofurkey (24), then subtract the number of guests who had both (12).

  16 + 24 − 12 = 28. Your answer is 28 total guests.

6. **0**

Set B has a large set of numbers, but because most of them are negative, you can't grid them in. The only positive values in set B are zero and 1. The number 1 is odd, but zero is an even integer. This makes zero the only intersection between sets A and B.

7. **25**

The Math Head on your shoulders should be able to convert the words in this stem into the following equation using the following key:

Term	Means
of	multiply
percent	divide by 100
is	equals

500% of 30% of 36 is what percent of 216?

$$\frac{500}{100} \times \frac{30}{100} \times 36 = \frac{n}{100} \times 216$$

$$5 \times \frac{3}{10} \times 36 = \frac{216n}{100}$$

$$54 = \frac{54n}{25}$$

$$\left(\frac{25}{54}\right)(54) = \frac{54n}{25}\left(\frac{25}{54}\right)$$

$$25 = n$$

The answer is 25.

8. **21**

Reluctantly and with a formal protest written into the log, we must answer a sequence item by doing the math. If there are seven consecutive integers, they could be written this way:

$$b$$
$$b + 1$$
$$b + 2$$
$$b + 3$$
$$b + 4$$
$$b + 5$$
$$b + 6$$

They each increase by one because that's the definition of *consecutive*. Because all seven integers equal 168 when added together, you have:

$$b + (b + 1) + (b + 2) + (b + 3) + (b + 4) + (b + 5) + (b + 6) = 168$$
$$7b + 21 = 168$$
$$7b = 147$$
$$b = 21$$

The lowest integer is 21.

9. **1/3**

How good is your memory? Things you learned on item 14 of the multiple-choice set can really help you here, because that is the item where you kept multiplying $-\frac{1}{2}$ by itself. On that item, you learned that most numbers get larger when you square them, unless they happen to be fractions between zero and 1 or zero and −1. For these fractions, the denominators swell when you square them, and a larger denominator makes a smaller fraction.

Let's try $^1/_3$ on this item.

$$x^3 > x^4$$
$$\left(\frac{1}{3}\right)^3 > \left(\frac{1}{3}\right)^4$$
$$\left(\frac{1}{3}\right)\left(\frac{1}{3}\right)\left(\frac{1}{3}\right) > \left(\frac{1}{3}\right)\left(\frac{1}{3}\right)\left(\frac{1}{3}\right)\left(\frac{1}{3}\right)$$
$$\frac{1}{27} > \frac{1}{81}$$

Any fraction between zero and 1 works.

10. **89**

You actually have two choices on how to solve this item:

1. You can find the total number of numbers between 1 and 49, then add to that all the numbers that have two digits.
2. You can determine how many numbers have one digit, then how many numbers have two digits, then add the two together.

Because we care, we are showing both. With method 1, there are 49 numbers total. (You can't subtract 49 − 1 and get 48 numbers because this would forget the 1 as a number.) Numbers 10 through 49 all have two digits—a units value and a tens value—and there are 40 of them in all:

$$49 + 40 = 89 \text{ total digits}$$

That's method 1. With method 2, we count up the number of single-digit numbers first:

$$1, 2, 3, 4, 5, 6, 7, 8, 9 = 9 \text{ digits}$$

Numbers 10 through 49 have two digits, and there are 40 of them, so the number of digits in the two-digit numbers is: $(2)(40) = 80$ digits.

$$80 + 9 = 89 \text{ digits}$$

Both methods, as you might expect, give you the value of 89.

11. **9**

Before you start multiplying all these numbers together, write them out first:

$$15 \times 16 \times 17 \times 18 \times 19 \times 20 \times 21 \times 22 \times \ldots \times 29 \times 30 =$$

The stem wants to know how many factors of 3 the end product will contain. Anything else is unimportant. For this reason, we can cull any numbers in the series that do not have 3 as a factor:

$$15 \times 18 \times 21 \times 24 \times 27 \times 30 =$$

There are six numbers to worry about. Before you rush off and grid in 6, however, make sure you know how many 3s are in the numbers above:

$$15 \times 18 \times 21 \times 24 \times 27 \times 30 =$$
$$(3 \times 5) \times (3 \times 6) \times (3 \times 7) \times (3 \times 8) \times (3 \times 9) \times (3 \times 10) =$$
$$(3 \times 5) \times (3 \times 3 \times 2) \times (3 \times 7) \times (3 \times 8) \times (3 \times 3 \times 3) \times (3 \times 10)$$

You can count the 3s in the equation above, or you can rearrange it the following way.

$$3 \times 3 \times 3 \times 3 \times 3 \times 3 \times 3 \times 3 \times 3 \times 2 \times 5 \times 7 \times 8 \times 10$$
$$= 3^9 \times 2 \times 5 \times 7 \times 8 \times 10$$

There are nine 3s, so the grid-in answer is 9.

12. **70**

This item makes you work every step of the way. If there are 150 students total and 1/3 of them bike, then 2/3 take the bus. 2/3 of 150 is 100:

150 students

50 bike, 100 take the bus

There are 45 boys in the class. If 15 of them bike, then 45 – 15 = 30 take the bus. You know that 100 total students take the bus, so 100 – 30 = 70 girls ride the bus.

13. **612**

You need to be a Supermath Head with sets and sequences for this item. Just sort of getting sequences and sets won't cut it.

An intersection of three sets is a number that appears in every set. Set T doesn't need much explaining, so let's focus on the other two. The stem states that set R consists of a geometric sequence where the first term is 17 and the constant ratio is 6. So start with 17 and start multiplying each subsequent term by 6:

Set $R = \{17, 102, 612, 3672, \ldots\}$

You can stop here because you've gone over 1,000, set T's upper limit. Set S is an arithmetic sequence, where you start with 87and add 175 to each subsequent term:

Set $S = \{87, 262, 437, 612, 787, 962, 1137, \ldots\}$

What number do these two sets have in common? 612. This is a positive integer less than 1,000, so it fits set T's description as well. The union is 612.

14. **1,299**

Let's take the stem and convert it into Mathspeak. If there are more blue pieces than red ones, then B > R. If there are more green pieces than blue, G > B. We can combine these two terms and write:

G > B > R

Now we add 1,000 red pieces to the mix:

G > B > 1,000

If there are 3,600 pieces total, the amount of blue and green pieces must be 3,600 – 1,000 = 2,600. Half of this number is 1,300. If green has 1,301 pieces and blue has 1,299 pieces, you have:

$$G > B > R$$

$$1,301 > 1,299 > 1,000$$

If you add any more to the blue pieces, the green pieces would no longer outnumber them. So 1,299 is the greatest number of blue pieces you can have.

15. **10.23**

There are three stages to this item, and each contains a potential trap. The first step consists of setting up a good table. Write out Days 1 through 10, then start filling things in:

Days	1	2	3	4	5	6	7	8	9	10
Money Saved	1	2	4	8	16	32	64	128	256	512

Some of you might grid in 512 or 5.12 at this point. Mistake. The stem wants to know how much Delilah saved, so you have to add everything up:

$$1 + 2 + 4 + 8 + 16 + 32 + 64 + 128 + 256 + 512 = 1,023$$

That was the second step. The third step is to convert this amount into dollars, because the stem asks for the amount in dollars. The answer in cents is 1,023, but 10.23 is the answer in dollars, so that's what you must grid in.

SPARKNOTES
Power Tactics for the New SAT

The Critical Reading Section
Reading Passages
Sentence Completions

The Math Section
Algebra
Data Analysis, Statistics & Probability
Geometry
Numbers & Operations

The Writing Section
The Essay
Multiple-Choice Questions: Identifying Sentence Errors,
Improving Sentences, Improving Paragraphs

The New SAT
Test-Taking Strategies
Vocabulary Builder